The Quotable Horse Lover

The Quotable
Horse Lover

EDITED BY STEVEN D. PRICE

THE LYONS PRESS
GUILFORD, CONNECTICUT
AN IMPRINT OF THE GLOBE PEQUOT PRESS

The Lyons Press is an imprint of The Globe Pequot Press.

Designed by Compset, Inc.

10 9 8 7 6 5 4

Library of Congress Cataloging-in-Publication Data

The quotable horse lover / [compiled by] Steven D. Price.
    p.   cm.
  ISBN 1-55821-950-1
  1. Horses Quotations, maxims, etc. I. Price, Steven D..

PN6084.H66Q68 1999
636.1—dc21   99-16537
                                                      CIP

Yet when all the books have been read and reread, it boils down to the horse, his human companion, and what goes on between them.

—WALTER FARLEY, AUTHOR OF *THE BLACK STALLION* SERIES, QUOTED IN *THE RANDOM HOUSE BOOK OF HORSES AND HORSEMANSHIP* BY PAULA RODENAS

By reading, riding and meditating, great results may be obtained, if there is true feeling for the horse and provided the rider's seat is good.

—NUNO OLIVEIRA, *REFLECTIONS ON EQUESTRIAN ART*

Contents

Introduction

What is it about horses that humans find so enthralling?

Trying to find answers to that age-old question was one reason for undertaking this book. Another was an excuse to spend countless hours delving into a wide variety of books, magazines, and other sources.

The task of rounding up a herd of horse-related quotations was made easier by a life surrounded by horse books. As an equestrian author and journalist, I'm also surrounded by riders, writers, and other friends and colleagues who generously suggested leads. Some were equally kind enough to contribute their own favorites. (And I must also acknowledge the World Wide Web, for its many useful sites and soundings.) Thanks to such help, finding candidates for inclusion was as easy as, well, as falling off a horse.

In no time at all, I became a horse-quotes junkie. Whether in person or by phone or e-mail, no one escaped being bombarded by my latest finds. And without the spur of meeting a deadline (and the publisher's dangling the carrot of a new fly-fishing rod if I delivered the manuscript on time), I'm sure I'd still be poring through bookstore or library stacks or squinting at the computer monitor in quest of yet one more quotation this book couldn't possibly live without.

Selecting the quotations was a more difficult task. Of the thousand-plus quotations under consideration, those that made the cut needed a special significance: a felicitous turn of phrase, an entertaining story, or a profound insight into the human/equine relationship. In more than a few instances, two or three of these criteria were met. Wherever practicable and relevant, a healthy chunk of the quotation lets readers see the context. Then too, a wide a range of cultures, eras, and activities confirm how universal and eternal the love of horses is.

Many quotations captured thoughts and feelings that friends, colleagues, and I have tried to express not only to each other but to ourselves.

As Alexander Pope suggested: "True wit is nature to advantage dressed/What oft was said, but ne'er so well expressed." Perhaps you'll find that some "ne'er so well expressed" entries motivate you to further reading. If you discover an insight into riding, training, or simply a new perspective about horses from anything here, imagine how much more you'll gain by exploring the full source in its original. Alas, too many of the books are out of print, but not all of them are, and a bit of time, effort, and ingenuity often pays off.

You may well come across an old friend or two: A poem, short story, novel, or another piece of literature you hadn't thought about in years. Those are friendships well worth renewing, and don't be surprised if you find that you appreciate the work even more with the passage of time.

You may be struck, as I was, by the range of people who had something to say about horses. Almost invariably, what they had to say was complimentary (Mark Twain being the most notable exception). It's an impressive array. Riders, trainers, and equestrian commentators stand alongside poets, novelists, and playwrights. "Anonymous" and "source unknown" are cheek by jowl to well-known literary and equestrian figures.

Horses don't know whether they're Thoroughbreds or Clydesdales or Shetlands, much less what sort of tack they're being ridden or driven under. All they care about is that they're horses. That's all we should too, at least for these purposes. In other words, don't shy from categories outside what you consider your own niches. No matter where your interests lie, there's much to be learned and enjoyed from people involved in any and all disciplines.

What, then, is it about horses that has inspired so much emotion from so many generations of so many cultures?

Although the quotations provide insights, there is no simple answer. The slices of prose and poetry that follow reflect diverse and often contradictory feelings of love, fear, awe, protectiveness, elation, frustration, companionship, and unalloyed joy. In short, the very same elements that forge relationships between humans and between humanity and the eternal.

And like the keys to these relationships, the secret of mankind's fascination with the horse will forever remain a divine mystery locked in our hearts.

———

On a personal note, two influences on my interest and involvement in horses must be acknowledged.

I never knew my maternal grandfather, Samuel Myiofis, but if there's anything to heredity, my love of horses comes from his contribution to the family gene pool.

An upholsterer by trade and living in Brooklyn, New York, Sam Myiofis made his deliveries by horse and wagon. His horses, all of whom received the name Baby, came from the West. He bought them at public auction, then patiently schooled them to harness and to such urban distractions as fire engines and elevated subways.

On Sundays and holidays, a buggy replaced the wagon, and the Baby of the period provided transportation for family outings. These horse-drawn excursions went on as late as the 1920s; owning a car held no charm or interest for my grandfather.

Not every Myiofis was such a horse lover, though. One of my grandfather's brothers bought a car, which precipitated an ongoing series of races along a broad avenue from Prospect Park to, several miles later, Coney Island. As family legend has it, Baby invariably won.

I wish I had known Sam Myiofis.

Anyone who has been a part of American equestrian life since the 1930s has benefited from the work of Alexander Mackay-Smith. A preeminent and prolific scholar, author, and editor, he also introduced a number of horse sports into this country and held important positions in many breed and discipline organizations.

Alex was a great friend and a caring mentor. A quote from George Eliot's *Adam Bede* reminds me of times we'd spend together: "The great advantage of a dialogue on horseback: it can be merged at any instant into a trot or canter, and one might escape from Socrates himself in the saddle." Alex and I would hack across the fields of his beloved Virginia foxhunting country, engrossed in discussing whatever project one or the other of us was currently involved in. But when a panel fence loomed ahead, the conversation was put on hold till we reached the other side. Notwithstanding George Eliot, there was no escaping from that particular Socrates—as if anyone would have wanted to.

I'm glad I knew Alex Mackay-Smith.

Steven D. Price
New York, New York
July 1999

The Quotable Horse Lover

Horses in Literature

I on my horse, and Love on me, doth try
Our horsemanships, while by strange work I prove
A horseman to my horse, a horse to Love,
And now man's wrongs in me, poor beast! decry.
The reins wherewith my rider doth me tie
Are humbled thoughts, which bit of reverence move,
Curb'd-in with fear, but with gilt bosse above
Of hope, which makes it seem fair to the eye:
The wand is will; thou, Fancy, saddle art,
Girt fast by Memory; and while I spur
My horse, he spurs with sharp desire my heart.
He sits me fast however I do stir,
And now hath made me to his hand so right,
That in the manage myself take delight.

—SIR PHILIP SIDNEY, "ASTROPHEL AND STELLA," SONNET IL

At one time the Horse had the plain entirely to himself. Then a Stag intruded into his domain and shared his pasture. The Horse, desiring to revenge himself on the stranger, asked a man if he were willing to help him in punishing the Stag. The man replied that if the Horse would receive a bit in his mouth and agree to carry him, he would contrive effective weapons against the Stag.

The Horse consented and allowed the man to mount him. From that hour he found that instead of obtaining revenge on the Stag, he had enslaved himself to the service of man.

—*AESOP'S FABLES*, THE HORSE AND THE STAG

When God created the horse He said to the magnificent creature: I have made thee as no other. All the treasures of the earth lie between thy eyes. Thou shalt carry my friends upon thy back. Thy saddle shall be the seat of prayers to me. And thou fly without wings, and conquer without any sword. Oh, horse.

—*THE KORAN*

Such horses are
The jewels of the horseman's hands and thighs,
They go by the word and hardly need the rein.
They bred such horses in Virginia then,
Horses that were remembered after death
And buried not so far from Christian ground
That if their sleeping riders should arise
They could not witch them from the earth again
And ride a printless course along the grass
With the old manage and light ease of hand.

—STEPHEN VINCENT BENÉT, *JOHN BROWN'S BODY*

The kites of olden times, as well as the swans, had the privilege of song. But having heard the neigh of the horse, they were so enchanted with the sound, that they tried to imitate it; and, in trying to neigh, they forgot how to sing.

Moral: The desire for imaginary benefits often involves the loss of present blessings.

—*AESOP'S FABLES*, THE KITES AND THE SWANS

———•◦•◦•———

Are you—poor, sick old ere your time—
Nearer one whit your own sublime
Than we who have never turned a rhyme?
Sing, riding's a joy!
For me, I ride.

—ROBERT BROWNING, "THE LAST RIDE TOGETHER"

. . . But why discourse
Upon the Virtues of the Horse?
They are too numerous to tell
Save when you have a Horse to Sell.

—JOSH BILLINGS [HENRY WHEELER SHAW],
JOSH BILLINGS: HIS SAYINGS

A horse that can count to ten is a remarkable horse, not a remarkable mathematician.

—SAMUEL JOHNSON, QUOTED IN *THE LIFE OF SAMUEL JOHNSON* BY
JAMES BOSWELL

They say princes learn no art truly, but the art of horsemanship. The reason is, the brave beast is no flatterer. He will throw a prince as soon as his groom.

—BEN JONSON, *EXPLORATA*

I give you horses for your games in May
And all of them well trained unto the course,
Each docile, swift, erect, a goodly horse;
With armour on their chests, and bells at play
Between their brows, and pennons fair and gay
Fine nets, and housings meet for warriors
Emblazoned with the shields ye claim for yours,
Gules, argent, or, all dizzy at noon day.

—ATTRIBUTED TO FOLGORE DI SAN GIMIGNANO

Four things greater than all things are—
Women and Horses and Power and War.

—RUDYARD KIPLING, "THE BALLAD OF THE KING'S JEST"

The horse, the horse! The symbol of surging potency and power of movement, of action, in man.

—D. H. LAWRENCE, *APOCALYPSE*

———•·•·•———

A short life in the saddle, Lord!
Not long life by the fire.

—LOUISE IMOGEN GUINEY, "THE KNIGHT ERRANT"

Women who ride, as a rule, ride better than men. They, the women, have always been instructed; whereas men have usually come to ride without any instruction. They are put upon ponies when they are all boys, and put themselves upon their fathers' horses as they become hobbledehoys: and thus they obtain the power of sticking on to the animal while he gallops and jumps, and even while he kicks and shies; and, so progressing, they achieve an amount of horsemanship which answers the purposes of life. But they do not acquire the art of riding with exactness, as women do, and rarely have such hands as a woman has on a horse's mouth.

The consequence of this is that women fall less often than men, and the field is not often thrown into the horror which would arise were a lady known to be in a ditch with a horse lying on her.

—ANTHONY TROLLOPE, *HUNTING SKETCHES*

Cast a cold eye
On life, on death.
Horseman, pass by!

—WILLIAM BUTLER YEATS, "UNDER BEN BULBEN" [THESE LINES ARE
INSCRIBED ON YEATS'S GRAVESTONE]

A horse is a vain thing for safety.

—PSALMS 33:17

The revolution does not choose its paths: it made its
first steps toward victory under the belly of a Cossack's
horse.

—LEON TROTSKY, *HISTORY OF THE RUSSIAN REVOLUTION*

I smell her still, I see her still, I hear the way she used to move about at night. What horse is ever so old as to forget his dam?

—JOHN HAWKES, *SWEET WILLIAM*

Yet if man, of all the Creator plann'd
His noblest work is reckoned,
Of the works of His hand, by sea or land,
The horse may at least rank second.

—ADAM LINDSAY GORDON, "HIPPODROMANIA"

It takes a good deal of physical courage to ride a horse. This, however, I have. I get it at about forty cents a flask, and take it as required.

—STEPHEN LEACOCK, "REFLECTIONS ON RIDING," *LITERARY LAPSES*

[He was] so learned that he could name a horse in nine languages ... So ignorant, that he bought a cow to ride on.

—BENJAMIN FRANKLIN

Who drives the horses of the sun
Shall lord it but a day.

—JOHN VANCE CHENEY, "THE HAPPIEST HEART"

The same philosophy is a good horse in the stable, but an arrant jade on a journey.

—OLIVER GOLDSMITH, "THE GOOD NATURED MAN"

Be not elated at any excellence that is not your own. If the horse in his elation were to say, "I am beautiful," it could be endured; but when you say in your elation, "I have a beautiful horse," rest assured that you are elated at something good that belongs to a horse.

—EPICTETUS, *DISCOURSES*

"Remember," he replied, "O perjur'd one,
The horse remember, that did teem with death,
And all the world be witness to thy guilt."

—DANTE, *THE INFERNO,* CANTO XXX

The Colonel's son has taken a horse, and a raw rough dun was he,
With the mouth of a bell and the heart of Hell
and the head of the gallows-tree.

—RUDYARD KIPLING, "THE BALLAD OF EAST AND WEST"

"You know, Doctor," said the horse, "that vet over the hill knows nothing at all. He has been treating me six weeks now—for spavins. What I need is SPECTACLES. I am going blind in one eye. There's no reason why horses shouldn't wear glasses, the same as people."

—HUGH LOFTING, *DOCTOR DOLITTLE*

The horses, mares, and frisking fillies,
Clad, all, in linen white as lilies.

—ROBERT HERRICK, "THE HOCK CART, OR HARVEST HOME"

Horses and men are just alike.
There was my stallion, Billy Lee,
Black as a cat and trim as a deer,
With an eye of fire, keen to start,
And he could hit the fastest speed
Of any racer around Spoon River.

—EDGAR LEE MASTERS, *SPOON RIVER ANTHOLOGY*

———

We should not even ignore those speculators on Reality
who doubted whether a white horse was real because
he was white, or because he was solid.

—KAKUZO OKAKURA, *THE BOOK OF TEA*

———

The love of horses which they had, alive,
And care of chariots, after death survive.

—VIRGIL, *THE AENEID*

O the horseman's and horsewoman's joys!
The saddle, the gallop, the pressure upon the seat, the
    cool gurgling by the ears and hair.

      —WALT WHITMAN, *LEAVES OF GRASS*

A monk there was, one made for mastery,
An outrider, who loved his venery;
A manly man, to be an abbot able.
Full many a blooded horse had he in stable:
And when he rode men might his bridle hear
A-jingling in the whistling wind as clear,
Aye, and as loud as does the chapel bell.

      —GEOFFREY CHAUCER, PROLOGUE TO *THE CANTERBURY TALES*

The whole world was made for man, but the twelfth part of man for woman. Man is the whole world, and the breath of God; woman the rib and crooked piece of man. I could be content that we might procreate like trees, without conjunction, or that there were any way to perpetuate the world without this trivial and vulgar way of coition: it is the foolishest act a wise man commits in all his life, nor is there anything that will more deject his cooled imagination, when he shall consider what an odd and unworthy piece of folly he hath committed. I speak not in prejudice, nor am averse from that sweet sex, but naturally amorous of all that is beautiful. I can look a whole day with delight upon a handsome picture, though it be but of an horse.

—SIR THOMAS BROWNE, *RELIGIO MEDICI*

Somewhere . . . Somewhere in time's Own Space
There must be some sweet pastured place
Where creeks sing on and tall trees grow
Some Paradise where horses go,
For by the love that guides my pen
I know great horses live again.

—STANLEY HARRISON

Dear to me is my bonnie white steed;
Oft has he helped me at pinch of need.

—SIR WALTER SCOTT, "ROKEBY"

It makes men imperious to sit a horse.

—OLIVER WENDELL HOLMES SR., *THE AUTOCRAT OF THE BREAKFAST TABLE*

Steeds, steeds, what steeds! Has the whirlwind a home in your manes?

—NIKOLAY GOGOL, *TARRAS BULBA*

'Orses and dorgs is some men's fancy. They're wittles and drink to me.

—CHARLES DICKENS, *DAVID COPPERFIELD*

Let the best horse leap the hedge first.

—THOMAS FULLER, M.D., *GNOMOLOGIA*

There is no need of spurs when a horse is running away.

—PUBLICUS SYRUS, *MORAL SAYINGS*

Go anywhere in England, where there are natural, wholesome, contented and really nice English people, and what do you always find? That the stables are the real centre of the household.

—GEORGE BERNARD SHAW, *HEARTBREAK HOUSE*

A good horse should be seldom spurred.

—THOMAS FULLER, M.D., *GNOMOLOGIA*

A lovely horse is always an experience . . . It is an emotional experience of the kind that is spoiled by words.

—BERYL MARKHAM, *WEST WITH THE NIGHT*

My horses understand me tolerably well; I converse with them at least four hours every day. They are strangers to bridle or saddle; they live in great amity with me, and friendship of each other.

—JONATHAN SWIFT, *GULLIVER'S TRAVELS*

And horses and mules and asses (hath He created) that ye may ride them, and for ornament. And He createth that which ye know not.

—*THE KORAN*

Lived in his saddle, loved the chase, the course,
And always, ere he mounted, kiss'd his horse.

—WILLIAM COWPER, "CONVERSATIONS"

While his rider every hand survey'd,
Sprung loose, and flew into an escapade;
Not moving forward, yet with every bound
Pressing, and seeming still to quit his ground.

—JOHN DRYDEN, "ABSALOM AND ACHITOPHEL"

What a creature he was! Never have I felt such a horse between my knees. His great haunches gathered under him with every stride, and he shot forward ever faster and faster, stretched like a greyhound, while the wind beat in my face and whistled past my ears.

—SIR ARTHUR CONAN DOYLE,
"THE ADVENTURES OF BRIGADIER GUARD"

With flowing tail and flying mane,
Wide nostrils, never stretched by pain,
Mouth bloodless to bit or rein,
And feet that iron never shod,
And flanks unscar'd by spur or rod.
A thousand horses—the wild—the free—
Like waves that follow o'er the sea,
Came thickly thundering on.

—GEORGE GORDON NOEL, LORD BYRON, "CHILDE HAROLD'S PILGRIMAGE"

A farmer's horse is never lame, never unfit to go. Never throws out curbs, never breaks down before or behind. Like his master he is never showy. He does not paw and prance, and arch his neck, and bid the world admire his beauties . . . and when he is wanted, he can always do his work.

—ANTHONY TROLLOPE, *HUNTING SKETCHES*

... he did not feel the ground under his feet ... he thrust himself into the capriole, rose high in the air ... forelegs and hindlegs horizontal. He soared above the ground, his head high in jubilation. Conquering!

—FELIX SALTEN, *FLORIAN*

I heard a neigh, Oh, such a brisk and melodious neigh it was. My very heart leaped with the sound.

—NATHANIEL HAWTHORNE

On horseback he seemed to require as many hands as a Hindu god, at least four for clutching the reins, and two more for patting the horse soothingly on the neck.

—H. H. MUNRO [SAKI]

Take most people, they're crazy about cars. I'd rather have a goddam horse. A horse is at least human, for godsake.

—J. D. SALINGER, *THE CATCHER IN THE RYE*

I love the horse from hoof to head.
From head to hoof and tail to mane.
I love the horse as I have said—
From head to hoof and back again.

—JAMES WHITCOMB RILEY, "I LOVE THE HORSE"

He flung himself on his horse and rode off madly in all directions.

—STEPHEN LEACOCK, *GUIDO THE GIMLET OF GHENT*

A fly, sir, may sting a stately horse, and make him wince; but one is still an insect, and the other a horse still.

—SAMUEL JOHNSON, ON CRITICS, AS QUOTED IN *THE LIFE OF SAMUEL JOHNSON* BY JAMES BOSWELL

He always looked a given horse in the mouth.

—FRANÇOIS RABELAIS, *MOTTEAUX'S LIFE*

I am sick as a horse.

—LAURENCE STERNE, *TRISTRAM SHANDY*

The Horse's Prayer—
I'm only a horse, dear Master, but my heart is warm
and true,
And I'm ready to work my hardest, for the pleasure of
pleasing you.
Good corn, and hay, and water, are all that I wish to
ask,
And a warm dry bed to rest on, when I've finished my
daily task.
Don't strike me in needless anger if I'm slow to
understand,
But encourage my drooping spirits with a gentle voice
and hand.
Finally, O my master! When my health and strength are
gone,
When I'm getting old and feeble, and my long life's
work is done,
Don't sell me to cruel owners, to be slaved to my latest
breath,

But grant me the untold blessing of a quick and
    painless death;
That, as you have always found me a patient and loyal
    friend,
The years of my faithful service may be crowned by a
    peaceful end.
I plead in the name of the Savior, Who cares when the
    sparrows fall.
Who was born in a lowly stable, and knows, and loves
    us all!

        —Anonymous, "The Horse's Prayer"

I pray that gentle hands may guide my feet;
I ask for kind commands from voices sweet;
At night a stable warm with scented hay,
Where, safe from every harm, I'll sleep till day.

—ANONYMOUS, "A PONY'S PRAYER"

He will hold thee, when his passion shall have spent its
novel force,
Something better than his dog, a little dearer than his
horse.

—ALFRED, LORD TENNYSON, "LOCKSLEY HALL"

Hobson's choice.
Tobias Hobson (died 1630) was the first man in England that let out hackney horses. When a man came for a horse he was led into the stable, where there was a great choice, but he obliged him to take the horse which stood next to the stable-door; so that every customer was alike well served according to his chance,—from whence it became a proverb when what ought to be your election was forced upon you, to say, "Hobson's choice."—Addison and Steele, *Spectator, No. 509.*

—*BARTLETT'S FAMILIAR QUOTATIONS* [1903 EDITION]

A dog starvd at his Master's Gate
Predicts the ruin of the State
A Horse misus'd upon the Road
Calls to Heaven for Human blood.

—WILLIAM BLAKE, "AUGURIES OF INNOCENCE"

Rider and horse—friend and foe—in one red burial blent!

—GEORGE GORDON NOEL, LORD BYRON,
"CHILDE HAROLD'S PILGRIMAGE"

The natives had never seen such horses up to this time and thought the horse and rider were all one animal.

—BERNARD DIAZ DEL CASTILLO,
TRUE HISTORY OF THE CONQUEST OF NEW SPAIN

Give a man a horse he can ride,
Give a man a boat he can sail;
And his rank and wealth, his strength and health,
On sea nor shore shall fail.

—JAMES THOMPSON, "SUNDAY UP THE RIVER"

But we most happy, who can fear no force
But winged troops, or Pegasean horse . . .

> —EDMUND WALLER, "TO THE KING ON HIS NAVY"

—•••—

I wheeled about,
Proud and exulting like an untired horse
That cares not for his home.

> —WILLIAM WORDSWORTH, "INFLUENCE OF NATURAL
> OBJECTS IN CALLING FORTH AND STRENGTHENING THE
> IMAGINATION IN BOYHOOD AND EARLY YOUTH"

Cannon to right of them,
Cannon to left of them,
Cannon behind them
Volley'd and thunder'd;
Storm'd at with shot and shell,
While horse and hero fell,
They that had fought so well
Came thro' the jaws of Death,
Back from the mouth of Hell,
All that was left of them,
Left of six hundred.

—ALFRED, LORD TENNYSON,
"THE CHARGE OF THE LIGHT BRIGADE"

And, even when she turn'd, the curse
Had fallen, and her future Lord
Was drown'd in passing thro' the ford,
Or kill'd in falling from his horse.

—ALFRED, LORD TENNYSON, "IN MEMORIAM: A. A. H."

The gravel'd ground, with sleeves tied on the helm,
On foaming horse, with swords and friendly hearts,
With cheer, as though the one should overwhelm

—HENRY HOWARD, EARL OF SURREY, "SO CRUEL PRISON"

Strong is the horse upon his speed;
Strong in pursuit the rapid glede,
Which makes at once his game . . .

—CHRISTOPHER SMART, "A SONG TO DAVID"

I have seen the general dare the combers come closer
And make to ride his bronze horse out into the hoofs
and guns of the storm.

—CARL SANDBURG, "BRONZES"

For, look you, my horse is good to prance
A right fair measure in this war-dance,
Before the eyes of Philip of France;
Ah! qu'elle est belle La Marguerite.

—WILLIAM MORRIS, "THE EVE OF CRECY"

And of the wond'rous horse of brass,
On which the Tartar king did ride . . .

—JOHN MILTON, "IL PENSEROSO"

We've had a stirring life, old woman!
You, and I, and the old grey horse.
Races, and fairs, and royal occasions.

—GEORGE MEREDITH, "JUGGLING JERRY"

True, a new mistress now I chase,
The first foe in the field;
And with a stronger faith embrace
A sword, a horse, a shield.

—RICHARD LOVELACE, "TO LUCASTA, GOING TO THE WARS"

Some men to carriages aspire;
On some the costly hansoms wait;
Some seek a fly, on job or hire;
Some mount the trotting steed, elate.

—AMY LEVY, "BALLADE OF AN OMNIBUS"

Then hey for boot and horse, lad,
And round the world away!
Young blood must have its course, lad,
And every dog his day.

—CHARLES KINGSLEY, "YOUNG AND OLD"

Honour to tight little John,
And the horse he rode upon!

—JOHN KEATS, "ROBIN HOOD"

What transport in her bosom grew,
When first the horse appear'd in view!

—JOHN GAY, "THE HARE AND MANY FRIENDS"

The pamper'd horse is seldom seen in breath,
Whose manger makes his grace (oftimes) to melt . . .

—GEORGE GASCOIGNE, "FIE! PLEASURE, FIE!"

My little horse must think it queer
To stop without a farmhouse near
Between the woods and frozen lake
The darkest evening of the year.

—ROBERT FROST, "STOPPING BY WOODS ON A SNOWY EVENING"

The fair Mariana sate watching a star,
When who should turn up but the young Lochinvar!
Her pulchritude gave him a pectoral glow,
And he reined up his hoss with stentorian "Whoa!"

—EUGENE FIELD, "AT CHEYENNE"

Think'st thou my wit shall keep the pack-horse way
That ev'ry dudgeon low invention goes?

—MICHAEL DRAYTON, "IDEA XXXI: METHINKS I SEE SOME
CROOKED MIMIC JEER"

Boot, saddle, to horse and away!
Rescue my castle before the hot day
Brightens to blue from its silvery gray,

(Chorus) *Boot, saddle, to horse, and away!*

—ROBERT BROWNING, "CAVALIER TUNES: BOOT AND SADDLE"

Nothing made the horse so fat as the king's eye.

—PLUTARCH, *LIFE OF CICERO*

To hear the horse neigh to the drum and trumpet, and
the trumpet and war shout reply.

—WILLIAM BLAKE, "THE FRENCH REVOLUTION"

And there lay the steed with his nostril all wide,
But through it there rolled not the breath of his pride;
And the foam of his gasping lay white on the turf,
And cold as the spray of the rock-beating surf.

—GEORGE GORDON NOEL, LORD BYRON,
"THE DESTRUCTION OF SENNACHERIB"

The Vizier proud, distinguish'd o'er the rest!
Six slaves in gay Attire his Bridle hold;
His Bridle rough with Gems, his Stirrups Gold;
His Snowy Steed adorn'd with lavish Pride
Whole Troops of Soldiers mounted by his Side,
These toss the Plumy Crest, Arabian Coursers guide.

—LADY MARY WORTLEY MONTAGU, "CONSTANTINOPLE"

He turn'd his charger as he spake,
Upon the river shore,
He gave his bridle-reins a shake,
Said, "Adieu for evermore,
My love!
And adieu for evermore."

—SIR WALTER SCOTT, "ROKEBY"

Fall, Hercules, from heaven, in tempests hurl'd,
And cleanse this beastly stable of the world . . .

—GEORGE CHAPMAN, "THE SHADOW OF NIGHT"

And neigh like Boanerges;
Then, punctual as a star,
Stop—docile and omnipotent—
At its own stable door.

—EMILY DICKINSON, "THE RAILWAY TRAIN"

Mother dear, we cannot stay!
The wild white horses foam and fret.

—MATTHEW ARNOLD, "THE FORSAKEN MERMAN"

As Bayard feels his oats, and in his pride
Begins to skip and sidle from his course
Until he feels the whiplash, then he thinks,
"Although I prance first in the tandom traces
Plumb and well groomed, still I am just a horse
I must put up with horses' law and pull
With other fellow creatures . . .

—GEOFFREY CHAUCER, "TROILUS AND CRESSIDA"

Tie the strings to my life, my Lord,
Then I am ready to go!
Just a look at the horses—
Rapid! That will do!

—EMILY DICKINSON, "TIE THE STRINGS TO MY LIFE, MY LORD"

Since then 'tis centuries; but each
Feels shorter than the day
I first surmised the horses' heads
Were toward eternity.

—EMILY DICKINSON, "THE CHARIOT
(BECAUSE I COULD NOT STOP FOR DEATH)"

To-night the very horses springing by
Toss gold from whitened nostrils.

—ARCHIBALD LAMPMAN, "WINTER EVENING"

One may lead a horse to water,
Twenty cannot make him drink.

—CHRISTINA ROSSETTI, "GOBLIN MARKET"

And that my Muse, to some ears not unsweet,
Tempers her words to trampling horses' feet
More oft than to a chamber melody.

—SIR PHILIP SIDNEY, "ASTROPHEL AND STELLA," SONNET VXXXIV

By the margin, willow veil'd,
Slide the heavy barges trail'd
By slow horses . . .

—ALFRED, LORD TENNYSON, "THE LADY OF SHALOTT"

But they must go, the time draws on,
And those white-favour'd horses wait;
They rise, but linger; it is late;
Farewell, we kiss, and they are gone.

—ALFRED, LORD TENNYSON, "IN MEMORIAM, O! LIVING WILL
THAT SHALT ENDURE"

I saw an aged Beggar in my walk;
And he was seated, by the highway side,
On a low structure of rude masonry
Built at the foot of a huge hill, that they
Who lead their horses down the steep rough road
May thence remount at ease.

—WILLIAM WORDSWORTH, "THE OLD CUMBERLAND BEGGAR"

O virgin, know'st thou not our steeds drink of the
    golden springs
Where Luvah doth renew his horses?

—WILLIAM BLAKE, "THE BOOK OF THEL"

And steeds, unbridled, sporting carelessly,
Crop the rank grass that on thy bosom grows . . .

—JOSEPH HOWE, "SABLE ISLAND"

So light to the croupe the fair lady he swung,
So light to the saddle before her he sprung!
"She is won! we are gone, over bank, bush, and scaur;
They'll have fleet steeds that follow,"quoth young
　　　Lochinvar.

　　　　　—SIR WALTER SCOTT, "MARMION"

As freely we rode on together
With helms unlaced and bridles slack.

　　　　　—WILLIAM MORRIS, "RIDING TOGETHER"

Ye old mule that think yourself so fair,
Leave off with craft your beauty to repair,
For it is true, without any fable,
No man setteth more by riding in your saddle.

　　　　　—SIR THOMAS WYATT, "YE OLD MULE"

Weel mounted on his grey mare, Meg,—
A better never lifted leg,—
Tam skelpit on thro' dub and mire,
Despising wind and rain and fire . . .

—ROBERT BURNS, "TAM O'SHANTER: A TALE"

His neck is high and erect, his head full with intelligence, his belly short, his back full, and his proud chest swell with hard muscle.

—VIRGIL, GEORGICS

A horse thou knowest, a man thou dost not know.

—ALFRED, LORD TENNYSON, IDYLLS OF THE KING,
"GARETH AND LYNETTE"

Mares, she said, had not been altered, in them the blood flowed freely, their life cycles had not been tampered with, their natures were completely their own. The mare usually had more energy than the gelding, could be as temperamental as the stallion and was, in fact, its superior.

—JOHN HAWKES, *WHISTLEJACKET*

The steeds soon perceived that the load they drew was lighter than usual; and as a ship without ballast is tossed hither and thither on the sea, so the chariot, without its accustomed weight, was dashed as if empty.

—*BULFINCH'S MYTHOLOGY*, "PHAETON"

And the hoofs of the horses as they run shakes the crumbling field.

—VIRGIL, *THE AENEID*

Whose only fit companion is his horse.

—WILLIAM COWPER, "CONVERSATIONS"

... when I looked at life from the saddle and was as near to heaven as it was possible to be.

—FRANCES, COUNTESS OF WARWICK, *DISCRETIONS*

Be it said in letters both bold and bright:
"Here is the steed that saved the day
By carrying Sheridan into the fight."

—THOMAS B. READ, "SHERIDAN'S RIDE"

Whose laughs are hearty, tho' his jests are coarse,
And loves you best of all things—but his horse.

—ALEXANDER POPE, "EPISTLE TO MRS. THERESA BLOUNT
ON HER LEAVING TOWN"

Every single movement of Florian's revealed nobility, grace, significance and distinction all in one; and in each of his poses he was the ideal model for a sculptor, the composite of all the equestrian statues in history.

—FELIX SALTEN, "FLORIAN"

. . . the mare . . . then set off for home with the speed of a swallow, and going as smoothly and silently. I never had dreamed of such delicate motion, fluent, and graceful, and ambient, soft as the breeze flitting over the flowers but swift as the summer lightning.

—R. D. BLACKMORE, LORNA DOONE

I think I learned this [not necessarily to follow the majority opinion] when, as a boy on horseback, my interest was not in the campus; it was beyond it; and I was dependent upon. Not the majority of boys, but myself and the small minority group that happened to have horses.

—LINCOLN STEFFENS, *THE AUTOBIOGRAPHY OF LINCOLN STEFFENS*

Their [the Tartars'] horses are so well broken-in to quick changes of movement, that upon the signal given, they instantly turn in every direction; and by these rapid manoeuvers many victories have been won.

—MARCO POLO, *THE DIVERSITIES AND MARVELS OF THE WORLD*

It was a glorious sight, and the come and go of the little, quick hooves, and the incessant salutations of ponies that had met before on other polo grounds or race-courses were enough to drive a four-footed thing wild.

—Rudyard Kipling, *The Maltese Cat*

It was a glorious sight, and the come and go of the little, quick hooves, and the incessant salutations of ponies that had met before on other polo grounds or race-courses were enough to drive a four-footed thing wild.

The horses of Achilles stood apart from their battle weeping, because they had learned that their charioteer had fallen in the dust by the hand of man-slaying Hector. When Zeus saw how they grieved, he took pity on them."Poor creatures, why did I give you to King Peleus, a mortal destined to die—you who are immortal."

—Homer, *The Iliad*

"The great art of riding, as I was saying, is to keep your balance properly. Like this, you know—" He let go the bridle and stretched out both his arms to show Alice what he meant, and this time he fell flat on his back, right under the horse's feet.

"Plenty of practice!" he went on repeating, all the time that Alice was getting him on his feet again.

—LEWIS CARROLL, *THROUGH THE LOOKING GLASS*

Ay, the horses trample,
The harness jingles now;
No change though you lie under
The land you used to plough.

—A. E. HOUSMAN, "A SHROPSHIRE LAD"

. . . but at Apollo's pleading
If that my Pegasus should not be founder'd,
I think to canter gently through a hundred.

—GEORGE GORDON NOEL, LORD BYRON, *DON JUAN*, CANTO TWELVE

Dosn't thou 'ear my 'erse's legs, as they canters away?
Proputty, proputty, proputty—that's what I 'ears 'em say.
Proputty, proputty, proputty—Sam, thou's an ass for
     thy pains:
Theer's moor sense i' one o' 'is legs, nor in all thy brains.

—ALFRED, LORD TENNYSON, "NORTHERN FARMER: NEW STYLE"

He quite forgot his holly whip,
And all his skill in horsemanship,

—WILLIAM WORDSWORTH AND SAMUEL TAYLOR COLERIDGE,
LYRICAL BALLADS, "THE IDIOT BOY"

"Bitzer," said Thomas Gradgrind. "Your definition of a horse."

"Quadruped. Graminivorous. Forty teeth, namely twenty-four grinders, four eye-teeth, and twelve incisive. Sheds coat in the spring; in marshy countries, sheds hoofs, too. Hoofs hard, but requiring to be shod with iron. Age known by marks in mouth."

"Now girl number twenty," said Mr. Gradgrind. "You know what a horse is."

—CHARLES DICKENS, *HARD TIMES*

Imagination is a good horse to carry you over the ground—not a flying carpet to set you free from improbability.

—ROBERTSON DAVIES, *THE MANTICORE*

Their land is full of horses,
There is no limit to their chariots.

—ISAIAH 2:7

It [the separation of the Baron's horse's hindquarters from its forequarters] would have been an irreparable loss, had not our farrier to bring both parts together while hot. He sewed them up with sprigs and young shoots of laurels that were at hand. The wound healed; and what could not have happened to so glorious a horse, the sprigs took root in his body, grew up and formed a bower over me, so that afterwards I could upon many other expeditions in the shade of my own and my horse's laurels.

—RUDOLPH RASPE, *THE TRAVELS OF BARON MUNCHAUSEN*

Poor little foal of an oppressed race!
I love the languid patience of thy face.

—Samuel Taylor Coleridge, "To a Young Ass"

When a harvester grows weary of his work, it is said "He has the fatigue of the Horse." The first sheaf, called the "Cross of the Horse," is placed on a cross of box-wood in the barn, and the youngest horse on the farm must tread on it.

—Sir James Frazer, The Golden Bough

Thou shall be for Man a source of happiness and wealth; thy back shall be a seat of honor, and thy belly of riches; every grain of barley given thee shall purchase indulgence for the sinner.

All the treasures of this earth lie between thine eyes. Thou shalt cast Mine enemies beneath thy hooves . . . This shall be the seat from whence prayers rise unto me.

—*THE KORAN*

Agesilaus was very fond of his children; and it is reported that once toying with them he got astride upon a reed as upon a horse, and rode about the room; and being seen by one of his friends, he desired him not to speak of it till he had children of his own.

—PLUTARCH, *LACONIC APOPHTHEGMS OF AGESILAUS THE GREAT*

For the Lord made the host of the Syrians to hear the noise of the chariots, and a noise of horses, even the noise of a great host.

—II KINGS 7:6

Show me a man who has no pity on his horse, and I will show you one who is a cruel husband, if he is married, and a tyrannical parent, if he has children; a man that would be Nero if he had the power. He is a coward by nature and a fiend by practice.

—GEORGE ELIOT, *MIDDLEMARCH*

When I was a child, I used to jump bareback over fences four to four and a half feet high. I don't remember being afraid. I think my mother took custody of the fear for me, and my job was only not to fall off and not to let on how often I was jumping. When I came back to riding at forty-four, though, every little two-foot fence looked to me like a Puissance wall.

—JANE SMILEY, "PUISSANCE," IN *HORSE PEOPLE,*
EDITED BY MICHAEL J. ROSEN

"What need I got for a horse I would need a bear trap to catch?" Eck said.

"Didn't you just see me catch him?"

"I seen you," Eck said. "And I don't want nothing as big as a horse if I got to wrastle with it every time it finds me on the same side of the fence it's on."

—WILLIAM FAULKNER, "SPOTTED HORSES"

Or on Pegasus mounted, well spurred and well booted,
With martingale fanciful, crupper poetic,
Saddle cloth airy, and whip energetic,
Girths woven of rainbows, and hard-twisted flax,
And horse-shoes as bright as the edge of an axe;
How blithe should she amble and prance on the road,
With a pillion behind.

—JOHN BRAINARD, *WRITTEN FOR A LADY'S COMMONPLACE-BOOK*

Don't know what to do to-day,
There's my fine new rocking-horse,
Long of tail and dapple-gray,
I *might* ride on him of course:
But my new velocipede—
What would *it* do then? or what
Would that"fiery, untamed steed,"
That I almost had forgot,
Hobbyhorse just think or say?—
Don't know what to do to-day.

—MADISON CAWAIN, "NOTHING TO DO"

Cicero said loud-bawling orators were driven by their weakness to noise, as lame men to take horse.

—PLUTARCH, *LIFE OF CICERO*

To battle rode George Washington
Upon my grandsire's courser,
And when the victory was won
The courser was no more, sir.

That faithful steed had borne our race
In saddle, chaise and pillion;
My father never saw his face,
But called him worth a million.

—J. W. DeForest, "Judge Boodle"

[Ayla] was thinking about naming the horse. I've never named anyone before. She smiled to herself. Wouldn't they think I was strange naming a horse. Not any stranger than living with one.

—Jean M. Auel, *The Valley of Horses*

No pity I ask, and no counsel I need,
But bring me, O, bring me, my gallant young steed,
With his high archèd neck, and his nostril spread wide,
His eye full of fire, and his step full of pride!
As I spring to his back, as I seize the strong rein,
The strength to my spirit returneth again!

—GRACE GREENWOOD, "THE HORSEBACK RIDE"

YOUTH, the circus-rider, fares gaily round the ring, standing with one foot on the bare-backed horse—the Ideal. Presently, at the moment of manhood, Life (exacting ring-master) causes another horse to be brought in who passes under the rider's legs, and ambles on. This is the Real. The young man takes up the reins, places a foot on each animal, and the business now becomes serious.

—SIDNEY LANIER, "AMBLING, AMBLING ROUND THE RING"

As I ride, as I ride
Ne'er has spur my swift horse plied,
Yet his hide, streaked and pied,
As I ride, as I ride,
Shows where sweat has sprung and dried,
—Zebra-footed, ostrich-thighed—
How has vied stride with stride
As I ride, as I ride!

—ROBERT BROWNING, "THROUGH THE METIDJA TO ABD-EL-KADR"

Right into the stars he reared aloft, his red eye rolling
    and raging,
He whirled and sunfished and lashed, and rocked the
    earth with thunder and flame.
He squealed like a regular devil horse. I was haggard
    and spent and aging—
Roped clean, but almost storming clear, his fury too
    fierce to tame.

—WILLIAM ROSE BENÉT, "THE HORSE THIEF"

When walkin' down a city street,
　　Two thousand miles from home,
The pavestone hurtin' of the feet
　　That never ought to roam,
A pony just reached to one side
　　And grabbed me by the clothes;
He smelled the sagebrush, durn his hide!
　　You bet a pony knows!

　　　　　—ARTHUR CHAPMAN, "THE MEETING"

Now the heart of a horse has love
For the master and home it knew:
And the mind of a horse can prove
That memory dwells there, too.

　　　　　—ELLA WHEELER WILCOX, "THE HORSE"

What are we, we your horses,
　　So loyal where we serve,
Fashioned of noble forces
　　All sensitive with nerve?
Torn, agonized, we wallow
　　On the blood-bemired sod;
And still the shiploads follow.
　　Have horses then no God?

> —KATHARINE LEE BATES, "THE HORSES" [THE POEM BEGINS WITH A
> HEADNOTE: "THUS FAR 80,000 HORSES HAVE BEEN SHIPPED FROM
> THE UNITED STATES TO THE EUROPEAN BELLIGERENTS"]

———•◦•———

Eager as fire though the last goal is won,
These wilding creatures gentled to the rein,
These little brothers of the wind and sun.

> —ELEANOR BALDWIN, "POLO PONIES"

Wherever thrumming hoofbeats drum
As galloping riders go or come;
Wherever a saddle is still a throne
And dust of hoofs by wind is blown;
Wherever are horsemen, young or old,
The Pacing Mustangs's tale is told.

—ANONYMOUS, "THE WHITE MUSTANG"

A little colt-broncho, loaned to the farm
To be broken in time without fury or harm,
Yet black crows flew past you, shouting alarm,
Calling "beware" with lugubrious singing . . .

—VACHEL LINDSAY, "THE BRONCHO THAT
WOULD NOT BE BROKEN"

For of this savage race unbent
The ocean is the element.
Of old escaped from Neptune's car, full sure
    Still with the white foam flick'd are they
    And when the seas puff black from gray,
    And ships part cables, loudly neigh
The stallions of the Camargue, all joyful in the roar.

    —GEORGE MEREDITH, "THE MARES OF THE CAMARGUE"

Let the Sultan bring his famous horses,
    Prancing with their diamond-studded reins;
They, my darling, shall not match thy fleetness
    When they course with thee the desert-plains.

    —BAYARD TAYLOR, "HASSAN TO HIS MARE"

First horse: We are the pets of men—
The pampered pets of men!
There is naught for us too gentle and good
In the graceful days of our babyhood.
They hang our portraits on their walls,
And paint and garnish and gild our stalls.

Second horse: We are the slaves of men—
The menial slaves of men! . . .
In the winds of Winter, or Summer sun,
The tread of our toil is never done . . .
They draft us into their bloody spites,
They spur us, bleeding, into their fights . . .

—WILLIAM "WILL" MCKENDREE CARLETON,
"DIALOGUE OF THE HORSES"

No honors wait him, medal, badge or star,
Though scarce could war a kindlier deed unfold;
He bears within his breast, more precious far
Beyond the gift of kings, a heart of gold.

—ANONYMOUS, "GOODBYE, OLD FRIEND" [INSPIRED BY AN
INCIDENT ON THE ROAD TO A BATTERY POSITION IN SOUTHERN
FLANDERS DURING WORLD WAR ONE]

With flowing tail and flying mane,
Wide nostrils never stretch'd by pain,
Mouths bloodless to the bit or rein,
And feet that iron never shod,
And flanks unscarr'd by spur or rod,
A thousand horse, the wild, the free,
Like waves that follow o'er the sea,
Came thickly thundering on . . .
They stop, they start, they snuff the air,
Gallop a moment here and there,
Approach, retire, wheel round and round . . .

—GEORGE GORDON NOEL, LORD BYRON, "MAZEPPA"

The roan horse is young and will learn: the roan horse buckles into harness and feels the foam on the collar at the end of a haul: the roan horse points four legs to the sky and rolls in the red clover . . .

—CARL SANDBURG, "POTATO BLOSSOM SONGS AND JIGS"

Behold! in glittering show,
A gorgeous car of state!
The white-plumed steeds, in cloth of gold,
Bow down beneath its weight;
And the noble war-horse, led
Caparison'd along,
Seems fiercely for his lord to ask,
As his red eye scans the throng.

—LYDIA HUNTLEY SIGOURNEY, "THE RETURN OF NAPOLEON FROM ST. HELENA"

MUSTANG, n. An indocile horse of the western plains. In English society, the American wife of an English nobleman.

—AMBROSE BIERCE, *THE DEVIL'S DICTIONARY*

The stallion flashed by the stands, going faster with every magnificent stride. With a sudden spurt he bore down on Sun Raider. For a moment he hesitated as he came alongside . . . Into the lead, the Black swept, past the cheering thousands—a step, a length, two lengths ahead—then the mighty giant plunged under the wire.

—WALTER FARLEY, *THE BLACK STALLION*

The animal that [Ichabod Crane] bestrode was a broken-down plow-horse that had outlived almost everything but its viciousness. He was gaunt and shagged, with a ewe neck, and a head like a hammer; his rusty mane and tail were tangled and knotted with burs; one eye had lost its pupil, and was glaring and spectral, but the other had the gleam of a genuine devil in it. Still he must have had fire and mettle in his day, if we may judge from the name he bore of Gunpowder.

—WASHINGTON IRVING, *THE LEGEND OF SLEEPY HOLLOW*

The thing about horses, he realized—and he never realized it until they were rolling on top of him in the dust, or rubbing him off against the side of a barn, trying to break his leg—was that if the horses didn't get broken, tamed, they'd just get wilder. There was nothing as wild as a horse that had never been broken. It just got meaner each day.

—RICK BASS, "WILD HORSES," IN *THE WATCH: STORIES*

Horses are not tamed by whips or blows. The strength of ten men is not so strong as a single strike of the hoof; the experience of ten men is not enough, for this is the unexpected, the unpredictable.

—BERYL MARKHAM, "THE SPLENDID OUTCAST," IN *THE SPLENDID OUTCAST: BERYL MARKHAM'S AFRICAN STORIES*

People, then, are not friend to horses unless their horses love them in return.

—PLATO, *LYSIS*

With his passion reverberating among the consonants like distant thunder, he laid his hand upon the mane of his horse as though it had been the gray locks of his adversary, swung himself into the saddle and galloped away.

—BRET HARTE, "THE RIGHT EYE OF THE COMMANDER"

The Union's too big a horse to keep changing the
    saddle
Each time it pinches you, As long as you're sure
The saddle fits, you're bound to put up with the pinches
And not keep fussing the horse.

    —STEPHEN VINCENT BENÉT, *JOHN BROWN'S BODY*

We attended stables, as we attended church, in our best
clothes, no doubt showing the degree of respect due to
horses, no less than to the deity.

    —SIR OSBERT SITWELL, *THE SCARLET TREE*

Take care to sell your horse before he dies. The art of life
is passing losses on.

    —ROBERT FROST, QUOTED IN *ROBERT FROST: A LIFE* BY JAY PARINI

[Robert Frost] was like a horse you could get along with if you came up beside him on the okay side.

—POET AND CRITIC ARCHIBALD MACLEISH, QUOTED IN *THE UNEASY CHAIR* BY WALLACE STEGNER

What the horses o' Kansas think today, the horses of America will think tomorrow; and I tell you that when the horses of America rise in their might, the day o' the Oppressor is ended.

—RUDYARD KIPLING, *THE DAY'S WORK*

So long as a man rides his hobbyhorse peaceably and quietly along the king's highway, and neither compels you or me to get up behind him—pray, sir, what have you or I to do with it?

—LAURENCE STERNE, *TRISTRAM SHANDY*

The great advantage of a dialogue on horseback: it can be merged at any instant into a trot or canter, and one might escape from Socrates himself in the saddle.

—GEORGE ELIOT, *ADAM BEDE*

There is nothing in which a horse's power is better revealed than in a neat, clean stop.

—MICHEL DE MONTAIGNE, QUOTED IN *SOME HORSES* BY THOMAS MCGUANE

With easy seat behold them ride—
These are the Truly qualified—
  Models of Sporting Men;
Graceful and elegant, yet neat;
Egad, the very sight's a treat
  I long to have again!

—SOURCE UNKNOWN, QUOTED IN *SPORTING PRINTS* BY F. L. WILDER

All in green went my love riding
On a great horse of gold
Into the silver dawn.

—E. E. CUMMINGS, "ALL IN GREEN WENT MY LOVE RIDING"

Lo! I knock the spurs away;
　Lo! I loosen belt and brand;
Hark! I hear the courser neigh
　For his stall in Fairy-land.

—WINTHROP MACKWORTH PRAED, "FAIRY SONG"

CENTAUR: One of a race of persons who lived before the division of labor had been carried to such a pitch of differentiation, and who followed the primitive economic maxim, "every man his own horse."

—AMBROSE BIERCE, *THE DEVIL'S DICTIONARY*

The gemmy bridle glitter'd free,
Like to some branch of stars we see
Hung in the golden Galaxy.
The bridle bells rang merrily
As he rode down to Camelot . . .

—ALFRED, LORD TENNYSON, "THE LADY OF SHALLOT"

And now ascends the nostril-stream
  Of stalwart horses come to plough.

—RICHARD HENRY HORNE, "THE PLOUGH"

But, snorting still with rage and fear,
He flew upon his far career;
At times I almost thought, indeed,
He must have slackened in his speed;
But no—my bound and slender frame
   Was nothing to his angry might,
And merely like a spur became.

—GEORGE GORDON NOEL, LORD BYRON, "MAZEPPA"

In India, Prince Siddhartha, who was to become the Buddah, took great pride in his magnificent stallion Kanthaka. When he left his home, he called for his noble animal and spoke to him as a friend. "Today I go forth to seek supreme beatitude; lend me your help, O Kanthaka! Companions in arms or in pleasure are not hard to find, and we never want for friends when we set out to acquire wealth, but companions and friends desert us when it is the path of holiness we would take.

"Yet of this I am certain: he who helps another to do good or to do evil shares in that good or in that evil. Know then, O Kanthaka, that it is a virtuous impulse that moves me. Lend me your strength and your speed. The world's salvation and your own is at stake."

—BRADLEY SMITH, *THE HORSE IN THE WEST*

You praise the firm restraint with which they write—
I'm with you there, of course:
They use the snaffle and the curb, all right,
But where's the bloody horse?

—ROY CAMPBELL, "ON SOME SOUTH AFRICAN NOVELISTS"

The tygers of wrath are wiser than the horses of
   instruction.

—WILLIAM BLAKE, SONGS OF INNOCENCE

A groom used to spend whole days in currycomb-
ing and rubbing down his Horse, but at the same time
stole his oats and sold them for his own profit. "Alas!"
said the Horse, "if you really wish me to be in good con-
dition, you should groom me less, and feed me more."

—AESOP'S FABLES, THE HORSE AND THE GROOM

What do we, as a nation, care about books? How much do you think we spend altogether on our libraries, public or private, as compared what we spend on our horses?

—JOHN RUSKIN, *SESAME AND LILIES*

Pat: He was an Anglo-Irishman.
Meg: In the blessed name of God, what's that?
Pat: A Protestant with a horse.

—BRENDAN BEHAN, *THE HOSTAGE*

Horse, thou art truly a creature without equal, for thou fliest without wings and conquerest without a sword.

—*THE KORAN*

Whenever the moon and stars are set,
Whenever the wind is high,
All night long in the dark and wet,
A man goes riding by.
Late in the night when the fires are out,
Why does he gallop and gallop about?

—ROBERT LOUIS STEVENSON, "WINDY NIGHTS," IN *A CHILD'S GARDEN OF VERSES*

From the desert I come to thee
On a stallion shod with fire,
And the winds are left behind
In the speed of my desire.

—BAYARD TAYLOR, "BEDOUIN SONG"

A hurry of hooves in a village street,
A shape in the moonlight, a bulk in the dark,
And beneath, from the pebbles, in passing, a spark
Struck out by a steed flying fearless and fleet.

—HENRY WADSWORTH LONGFELLOW, "THE MIDNIGHT RIDE OF
PAUL REVERE"

Oh wasn't it naughty of Smudges?
Oh, Mummy, I'm sick with disgust.
She threw me in front of the Judges,
And my silly old collarbone's bust.

—SIR JOHN BETJEMAN, "HUNTER TRIALS"

He wheels his horse with a touch,
sword in hand.
How exquisite.

—A HAIKU BY YOSHIMOTO

Her hooves fly faster than every flies the whirlwind,
Her tail-bone borne aloft, yet the hairs sweep the ground.

—ANONYMOUS ARABIAN POET, "THE IDEAL HORSE"

Stood up in the stirrups, leaned, patted his ear,
Called my Roland his pet-names, my horse without
    peer—
Clapped my hands, laughed and sang, any noise, bad or
    good,
Till at length into Aix Roland galloped and stood.

—ROBERT BROWNING, "HOW THEY BROUGHT THE GOOD NEWS
FROM GHENT TO AIX"

[And this parody:]

I unsaddled the saddle, unbuckled the bit,
Unshackled the bridle (the bit didn't fit)
And ungalloped, ungalloped, ungalloped, ungalloped
    a bit.

—R. J. YEATMAN AND W. C. SELLAR, "HOW I BROUGHT THE GOOD
NEWS FROM AIX TO GHENT (OR VICE VERSA)"

Horse People may be heads of state or professionally un-
employed in their private lives, but horses are their passion,
as Jerusalem was the passion of a soldier in some ancient
crusade. The cult of the horse as their idol is as central to
their lives as cocaine is to some and applause is to others.

—JUDITH KRANTZ, *PRINCESS DAISY*

Spur not an unbroken horse.

—SIR WALTER SCOTT, *THE MONASTERY*

A small, select aristocracy, born booted and spurred to ride, and a large dim mass born saddled and bridled to be ridden.

—A. G. GARDINER, PROPHETS, PRIESTS AND KINGS [THE REFERENCE IS TO GREAT BRITAIN BEFORE WORLD WAR ONE]

I saw him out riding in the Row, clutching to his horse like a string of onions.

—MARGOT ASQUITH, THE AUTOBIOGRAPHY OF MARGOT ASQUITH

Horse: A neighing quadruped, used in war, and draught and carriage.

—SAMUEL JOHNSON, DICTIONARY OF THE ENGLISH LANGUAGE

The day was as hot as the sun on a bay horse's back.

—VERLYN KLINKENBORG, "GRATITUDE: WHEN CONTENTEDNESS COMES HOME"

The Scythian cavalry regiments indeed resound with famous stories of horses: a chieftain was challenged to a duel by an enemy and killed, and when his adversary came to strip his body of his armor, his horse kicked him and bit him till he died; another horse, when his blinkers were removed and it found out that the mare he had covered was his dam, made for a precipice and committed suicide.

—PLINY THE ELDER, *NATURAL HISTORY*

The old grey horse, dreaming as he plodded along, of his quiet paddock, in a new raw situation such as this simply abandoned himself to his natural emotions. Rearing, plunging, backing steadily, in spite of all the Mole's efforts at his head, and all the Mole's lively language directed at his better feelings, he drove the cart backwards towards the deep ditch at the side of the road.

—KENNETH GRAHAME, *THE WIND IN THE WILLOWS*

The steed bit his master;
How came this to pass?
He heard the good pastor
Cry, "All flesh is grass."

—ANONYMOUS, "ON A CLERGYMAN'S HORSE BITING HIM"

The rider
Is fat
As that ( )
Or wider ( )
In torso
Of course
The horse
Is more so ( )

—WEY ROBINSON, "HORSE & RIDER"

Or if we rode, perhaps she *did*
Pull sharply at the curb;
But the way in which she slid
From horseback was superb!

—C. S. CALVERLEY

They head the list
Of bad to bet on,
But I insist
They're worse to get on.

—RICHARD ARMOUR, "HORSES"

No gymnastics could be better or harder exercise, and this and the art of riding, are of all the arts the most befitting a free man . . .

—PLATO, *LACHES*

You can't control a young horse unless you can control yourself.

—LINCOLN STEFFENS, *THE AUTOBIOGRAPHY OF LINCOLN STEFFENS*

Must we drag on this stupid existence forever,
So idly and weary, so full of remorse,
While everyone else takes his pleasure, and never
Seems happy unless he is riding a horse?

—EDWARD LEAR, *LAUGHABLE LYRICS*

As judges of horseflesh they [the Irish tinkers] are hard to beat, and make their living trading horses or "finding" them before the owner has lost them.

—DOROTHEA DONN BYRNE, *THE TURN OF THE WHEEL*

Jess stopped laughing but said nothing. He figured Eliza had gone about as far in one day as a woman could in enlarging her appreciation of horseflesh; still he couldn't help smiling when he thought of the sermon that might have been preached in the Bethel Church upon eternal verities.

—JESSAMYN WEST, *FRIENDLY PERSUASION*

Some people object to high-blowers, that is, 'osses wot make a noice like steam-engines as they go. I don't see no great objection to them myself, and think the use they are of clearin' the way in crowded thoroughfares, and the protection they afford in dark night by pre-ventin' people ridin' against you, more than counterbal-ance any disconvenience.

—ROBERT SMITH SURTEES [JOHN JORROCK], *HANDLEY CROSS*

As a boy in a prairie town I early learned to revere the work horse. To me, as to all boys, a dog was a slave, but a horse was a hero. And the men who handled him were heroes too.

—JAMES STEVENS, *HORSES*

———

Now whether the tall horse, in the natural playfulness of his disposition, was desirous of having a little innocent recreation with Mr. Winkle, or whether it occurred to him that he could perform the journey as much to his own satisfaction without a rider as with one, are points upon which, of course, we can arrive at no distinct conclusion.

—CHARLES DICKENS, *THE PICKWICK PAPERS*

Then there was the bridle. Billy explained how to use a stick of licorice for a bit until Galiban was used to having something in his mouth. Billy explained, "Of course we could force-break him to everything, but he wouldn't be as good a horse if we did. He'd always be a bit afraid, and he wouldn't mind because he wanted to."

—JOHN STEINBECK, *THE RED PONY*

"Will you lend me your mare to go a mile?"
"No, she is lame leaping over a stile."
"But if you will her to me spare,
You should have money for your mare."
"Oh ho, say you so?
Money will make the mare go."

—OLD ENGLISH SONG

The Associated Press reports carrying the news of Mary White's death declared that it came as a result from the fall from a horse. How she would have hooted at that! She never fell from a horse in her life. Horses have fallen on her and with her—"I'm always trying to hold 'em in my lap," she used to say. But she was proud of few things, and one was that she could ride anything that had four legs and hair.

—WILLIAM ALLEN WHITE, "MARY WHITE" [THE NEWSPAPER EDITOR'S OBITUARY FOR HIS DAUGHTER]

I'm Captain Jinx of the Horse Marines,
I feed my horse on corn and beans,
And often life beyond my means,
  Though a captain in the army.

—ANONYMOUS, "CAPTAIN JINX OF THE HORSE MARINES"

Now the world is white, go it while you're young,
Take the girls tonight, and sing this sleighing song:
Just get a bob-tailed nag, two-forty for his speed,
Then hitch him to an open sleigh, and crack! You'll take
   the lead.

—J. PIERPONT, "JINGLE BELLS" ["TWO-FORTY" REFERS TO THE TIME
THE HORSE WOULD TROT A MILE]

Remember, a horse can tell you a lot of things, if you
watch, and expect it to be sensible and intelligent.

—MARY O'HARA, MY FRIEND FLICKA

A man in passion rides a mad horse.

—BENJAMIN FRANKLIN, POOR RICHARD'S ALMANACK

In Aberdeenshire the last sheaf [of wheat] or "Maiden" is carried home in merry procession by the harvesters. It is then presented to the mistress of the house, who dresses it up to be preserved until the first mare foals. The Maiden is then taken down and presented to the mare as its first food. The neglect of this would have untoward effects upon the foal.

—SIR JAMES FRAZER, *THE GOLDEN BOUGH*

The stallion Eternity
Mounted the mare of Time
'Gat the foal of the world.

—WILLIAM BUTLER YEATS, "TOM AT CRUACHAN"

Come off to the stable, all you who are able,
And give your horses some oats and some corn;
For if you don't do it, your colonel will know it,
And then you will rue it, as sure as you're born.

—WORDS TO THE "STABLE CALL" CAVALRY BUGLE CALL

Ay, they heard his foot upon the stirrup,
And the sound of iron on stone
And how the silence surged softly backward
When the plunging hoofs were gone.

—WALTER DE LA MARE, "THE LISTENERS"

Let me leap into the saddle once more.

—HERMAN MELVILLE, *WHITE JACKET*

Powerful loin, and quarter wide,
Grace and majesty allied,
Basic power—living force—
Equine king—the Clydesdale horse.

—ANONYMOUS, "THE CLYDESDALE HORSE"

He [Rumbold] never would believe that Providence had sent a few men into the world ready booted and spurred to ride, and millions ready saddled and bridled to be ridden.

—THOMAS BABINGTON MACAULAY, *HISTORY OF ENGLAND*

I had a little pony,
His name was Dapple Gray;
I lent him to a lady
To ride a mile away;
She whipped him, she slashed him,
She rode him through the mire;
I would not lend my pony now
For all the lady's hire.

—Anonymous, "I Had a Little Pony"

So hurry to see your lady,
Like a stallion on the track.

—anonymous love song of the New Kingdom of ancient Egypt

Shoe the horse, shoe the mare,
But let the little horse go bare.

—Anonymous, "Shoe the Horse"

He that makes an ass of himself must not take it ill if men ride him.

—THOMAS FULLER, M.D., *GNOMOLOGIA*

———•◦•◦•———

In his day he had been a star on the Georgia Tech football team. Football had left him with a banged-up right knee, that had turned arthritic about three years ago ... One of the beauties of the Tennessee walking horse was that its gait spared you from having to post, to pump up and down at the knees when the horse trotted. He wasn't sure he could take posting on this chilly February morning.

—TOM WOLFE, *A MAN IN FULL*

And here I say to parents, and especially to wealthy parents, Don't give your son money. As far as you can afford it, give him horses. No one ever came to grief—except honourable grief—through riding horses. No hour of life is lost that is spent in the saddle. Young men have often been ruined through owning horses, or through backing horses, but never through riding them; unless of course they break their necks, which, taken at a gallop, is a very good death to die.

—SIR WINSTON CHURCHILL, *My Early Life*

The merchant serves the purse,
The eater serves his meat;
T is the day of the chattel,
Web to weave, and corn to grind;
Things are in the saddle,
And ride mankind.

—RALPH WALDO EMERSON, "ODE (INSCRIBED TO W. H. CHANNING)"

"Ain't you never heard what Peter done?
Run the quarter-mile in twenty-one
And he run it backwards in twenty flat;
Why, stranger, where have you been at?"
    "What else could he do,
    This Peter McCue?"
"He could gallop the range with tireless legs,
He could build a fire and scramble the eggs;
Though he never learned to subtract or divide,
He was mighty good when he multiplied."

—ANONYMOUS, "PETER MCCUE" [CELEBRATING THE VERSATILITY OF A NINETEENTH-CENTURY QUARTER HORSE]

Love animals. God has given them the rudiments of thought and joy untroubled. Do not trouble their joy, do not harass them, do not deprive them of their happiness, do not work against God's intention.

—FYODOR DOSTOYEVSKY, THE BROTHERS KARAMAZOV

For never man had friend
More enduring to the end,
Truer mate in every turn of time and tide.
Could I think we'd meet again
It would lighten half my pain?
At the place where the old horse died.

—G. J. WHYTE-MELVILLE,
"THE PLACE WHERE THE OLD HORSE DIED"

The colt in the Long Meadow kicked up his heels.
"That was a fly," he thought. "It's early for flies."
But being alive, in April, was too fine
For flies or anything else to bother a colt.
He kicked up his heels again, this time in pure joy,
And started to run a race with the wind and his
    shadow.

—STEPHEN VINCENT BENÉT, *JOHN BROWN'S BODY*

And he arched his neck, so graceful, and he tossed his
    tail, so saucy,
Like a proudly waving plume long and black!

He was light of hoof and fleet, I was supple, firm in
    seat,
And no sort of thing with feet, anywhere
In the country, could come nigh us; scarce the swallows
    could outfly us;
But the planet spun beneath us, and the sky went
    whizzing by us,
In the hurricane we made of the air.

—ROBERT W. SERVICE, "OLD ROBIN"

A bad-tempered man will never make a good-tempered
horse.

—ANNA SEWELL, *BLACK BEAUTY*

You hear of the city feller who wanted to board his horse and he asked his friends what he ought to pay and they said, "The price ranges from one dollar a month to fifty cents to two bits, but whatever you pay you're entitled to the manure."

So this city feller goes to the first farmer, and the farmer says, "One dollar," and the city feller said, "But I get the manure?" The farmer nods, and at the next place it's fifty cents, and the city feller says, "But I get the manure?" and the farmer nods.

At the third farm two-bits and the same story, so the city feller says, "Maybe I can find a place that's real cheap," and he goes to a broken-down farm and the man says, "Ten cents a month," and the city feller says, "But I get the manure?" and the farmer says, "Son, at ten cents a month there ain't gonna be any manure."

—JAMES MICHENER, *CENTENNIAL*

So turning to his horse, he said,
I am in haste to dine;
'Twas for your pleasure you came here,
You shall go back for mine.

—WILLIAM COWPER, "JOHN GILPIN"

The mare soon after my entrance rose from her mat, and coming up close, after having nicely observed my hands and face, gave me the most contemptuous look, and turning to the horse, I heard the word *Yahoo* often repeated twixt them; the meaning of which I could not comprehend.

—JONATHAN SWIFT, *GULLIVER'S TRAVELS*

England is the paradise of women, the purgatory of men, and the hell of horses.

—JOHN FLORIO, "SECOND FRUTES"

Men are generally more careful of the breeding of their horses and dogs than of their children.

—WILLIAM PENN, "SOME FRUITS OF SOLITUDE, IN REFLECTIONS AND MAXIMS RELATING TO THE CONDUCT OF HUMAN LIFE"

And I looked, and beheld a pale horse: and his name that sat upon him was Death, and Hell followed with him.

—REVELATION 6:8

Suppose . . . and suppose that a wild little Horse of Magic
   Came cantering out of the sky,
With bridle of silver and into the saddle I mounted
   To fly—and to fly.

—WALTER DE LA MARE, "SUPPOSE"

Once more upon the water, yet once more!
And the waves bound beneath me as a steed
That knows his rider!

  —GEORGE GORDON NOEL, LORD BYRON,
  "CHILDE HAROLD'S PILGRIMAGE"

Lo, the Turquoise Horse of Johano-ai . . .
There he spurns dust of glittering grain—
How joyous his neigh.

  —NAVAJO SONG OF THE HORSE

I love the disciplined panic of a horse flirting with a
tantrum at every turn, the delicate voluptuous play or
muscles, the grace-sprung power.

  —DIANE ACKERMAN, "ASTRIDE THE TWILIGHT," IN *HORSE PEOPLE,*
  EDITED BY MICHAEL J. ROSEN

What delight to back the flying steed that challenges the wind for speed! . . . Whose soul is in his task, turns labour into sport!

—James Sheridan Knowles

———

But he, mighty man, lay mightily in the whirl of dust, forgetful of his horsemanship.

—Homer, *The Iliad*

———

The ego's relation to the id might be compared to that of the rider to his horse. The horse supplies the locomotive energy, while the rider has the privilege of deciding on the goal and of guiding the powerful animal's movement.

—Sigmund Freud, *New Introductory Lectures on Psycho-Analysis*

What is the price of a thousand horses against a son when there is one son only?

—JOHN MILLINGTON SYNGE, *RIDERS TO THE SEA*

My beautiful! my beautiful!
  That standeth meekly by
With thy proudly arch'd and glossy neck,
  And dark and fiery eye;
The stranger hath they bridle-rein,
  Thy master hath his gold;
Fleet limbed and beautiful, farewell;
  Thou'rt sold; my steed, thou'rt sold.

—CAROLINE ELIZABETH SHERIDAN NORTON, "THE ARAB'S FAREWELL TO HIS STEED"

Ah, the nag you so disdain, with his scanty tail and mane,
And that ridge-pole to shed rain, called a back,
Then was taper-limbed and glossy,—so superb a creature
    was he!
I hear an army charging upon the land,
And the thunder of horses plunging, foam about their
    knees:
Arrogant, in black armour, behind them stand,
Disdaining the reins, with fluttering whips, the charioteers.

      —JAMES JOYCE, "I HEAR AN ARMY"

—•••—

  Horses: the feeling of the absolute ancientness of the English landscape. A landscape that should always, by rights, have horses in it.

  So, too, should the landscape of the English mind.

      —SIMON BARNES, "ENTHRALLED BY THE VIEW FROM JASPER'S
      BACK" IN THE *TIMES* (LONDON), MAY 29, 1999

She doted upon the Assyrians her neighbours, captains and rulers clothed most gorgeously, horsemen riding upon horses, all of them desirable young men.

—EZEKIEL 23:12

Stone, bronze, stone, steel, stone, oakleaves,
  Horses' heels
Over the paving.

—T. S. ELIOT, "CORIOLON I: TRIUMPHAL MARCH"

Content with harmless sport and simple food,
Boundless in faith and love and gratitude;
Happy the man, if there be any such—
Of whom his epitaph can say as much.

—ROBERT LOWE, LORD SHERBROOKE, "A HORSE'S EPITAPH"

Where in this world can man find nobility without pride, friendship without envy, beauty without vanity? Here, where grace is laced with muscle, and strength by gentleness confined. He serves without servility; he has fought without enmity. There is nothing so powerful, nothing less violent; there is nothing so quick, nothing more patient. England's past has been borne on his back. All our history is his industry: we are his heirs, he is our inheritance. Ladies and gentlemen: The Horse!

—ROBERT DUNCAN'S "TRIBUTE TO THE HORSE" [READ AT THE CONCLUSION OF EVERY HORSE OF THE YEAR SHOW IN LONDON]

2

Riding and Training

It's what you learn after you know it all that's important.
—LEGENDARY CALIFORNIA RIDER AND TRAINER JIMMY WILLIAMS

Riding is simple . . . it's just not easy.
—ANONYMOUS

Know what you're going to have to do, and allow yourself plenty of time to do it in.
—WILLIAM STEINKRAUS, *RIDING AND JUMPING*

Some people think horses are dumb. Ability and intelligence are in all horses, regardless of breed. Their so-called stupidity stems from our poor communication. Training a horse is like drawing a picture. The better I draw the picture, the better the communication. If I'm drawing a horse in pencil, I've communicated something. If I add crayon to my drawing, you can then tell that the horse I've drawn is a Palomino. Does that mean that you've gotten smarter? No. It means that I've become a better communicator.

—JOHN LYONS, WITH SINCLAIR BROWN, *LYONS ON HORSES*

Another behavior that is breed-specific is homing ability which, while present in other breeds, is legendary in Icelandic ponies. Why the equines of a northern island should have a refined talent for finding their way home is not clear.

—PAUL MCGREEVY, *WHY DOES MY HORSE . . . ?*

Intimate acquaintance with the horse's knowledge and leading the kind of life that entails the continual reimaginings of horsemanship mark the faces of some older riders with the look that I have also seen on the faces of a few poets and thinkers, the incandescent gaze of unmediated awareness that one might be tempted to call innocence, since it is not unlike the gaze on the face of a child absorbed in Tinkertoys or a beautiful bug, but it is an achieved or restored innocence, and it is also terrible, the way Pasternak's face was terrible in its continuing steadiness of gaze.

—VICKI HERNE, *ADAM'S TASK*

We quickly learned that Max [Uncle Max, Shapiro's show jumper] possessed several serious quirks which we would need to iron out. My number one problem was mounting. As soon as Max knew I was aiming for the saddle, he would be off and running. We decided that the element of surprise would be our only hope. It was not uncommon to see me leaping onto the saddle from the hood of a car, a bale of hay or even a rooftop.

—OLYMPIC SHOW-JUMPING RIDER NEAL SHAPIRO, "FROM UNCLE MAX TO A MEDAL," IN *THE U.S. EQUESTRIAN TEAM BOOK OF RIDING*, EDITED BY WILLIAM STEINKRAUS

When riding a high-strung horse, pretend you are riding an old one.

—DOMINIQUE BARBIER, *SOUVENIRS*

As one of the famous d'Inzeo brothers, riders on the Italian jumping team at the Rome Olympics, was quoted as saying, "The mastery of a perfect technique takes a lifetime. Technical mastery is merely sufficient for you to become good; it is not enough to make you great. From excellence to greatness, a man is alone. He must count on imponderables—his own instinctive resources, his character and his secret gifts. They are never the same for two people, not even for brothers."

—OLYMPIC EVENTER MICHAEL O. PAGE, "THE EDUCATION OF A THREE DAY RIDER," IN *THE U.S. EQUESTRIAN TEAM BOOK OF RIDING*, EDITED BY WILLIAM STEINKRAUS

If one induces the horse to assume that carriage which it would adopt of its own accord when displaying its beauty, then, one directs the horse to appear joyous and magnificent, proud and remarkable for having been ridden.

—XENOPHON, *ON HORSEMANSHIP*

Teaching a horse to jump fences is more like instructing a child to read than like training a dog to stay or fetch.

—HOLLY MENINO, *FORWARD MOTION*

———•·•·•———

What does it take to train a horse? More time than the horse has.

—FORMER ALL-AROUND RODEO CHAMPION LARRY MAHAN

———•·•·•———

Anything forced and misunderstood can never be beautiful. And to quote the words of Simon: If a dancer was forced to dance by whip and spikes, he would be no more beautiful than a horse trained under similar conditions.

—XENOPHON, 400 B.C.

Every time you ride, you're either teaching or un-teaching your horse.

—GORDON WRIGHT

———•·•·•———

There are many forms of riding. The classical way, however, reaches back centuries and has proved to be the right one. When following it, one realises that it is a very open way of schooling. It is a wide road that accommodates every horse.

—ARTHUR KOTTAS-HELDENBERG, QUOTED IN *VISIONS OF DRESSAGE* BY ELIZABETH FURST

What is it that makes horses give their rider everything? It can only be a reaction based on mutual trust. Once a horse trusts his partner, he develops and grows; and once a rider has found trust in his horse's abilities, he can develop the confidence needed to achieve special accomplishments.

—ELIZABETH FURST, *VISIONS OF SHOW JUMPING*

Riding is a partnership. The horse lends you his strength, speed and grace, which are greater than yours. For your part you give him your guidance, intelligence and understanding, which are greater than his. Together you can achieve a richness that alone neither can.

—LUCY REES, *THE HORSE'S MIND*

To make a perfect horseman, three things are requisite. First, to know how and when to help your horse. Secondly, how and when to correct him. And thirdly, how and when to praise him and to make much of him.

—THOMAS BLUNDEVILLE

Half the failures in life arise from pulling in one's horse as he is leaping.

—JULIUS AND AUGUSTUS HARE, *GUESSES AT TRUTH*

The horse you get off is not the same as the horse you got on; it is your job as a rider to ensure that as often as possible the change is for the better.

—ANONYMOUS

A good trainer can hear a horse speak to him. A great trainer can hear him whisper.

—MONTY ROBERTS, *THE MAN WHO LISTENS TO HORSES*

I don't help people with horse problems, I help horses with people problems.

—NICHOLAS EVANS, *THE HORSE WHISPERER*

A horseman should know neither fear, nor anger.

—ATTRIBUTED TO JAMES RAREY

An extra pressure, a silent rebuke, an unseen praising, a firm correction: all these passed between us as through telegraph wires.

—CHRISTILOT HANSON BOYLEN

The one best precept—the golden rule in dealing with a horse—is never to approach him angrily. Anger is so devoid of forethought that it will often drive a man to do things which in a calmer mood he will regret.

—XENOPHON, *ON HORSEMANSHIP*

It's a lot like nuts and bolts—if the rider's nuts, the horse bolts!

—NICOLAS EVANS, *THE HORSE WHISPERER*

It is the best of lessons if the horse gets a season of repose whenever he has behaved to his rider's satisfaction.

—XENOPHON, *ON HORSEMANSHIP*

———

The great want in a man's seat is firmness, which would be still more difficult for a woman to acquire if she rode in a cross-saddle, because her thighs are rounder and weaker than those of a man. Discussion of this subject is, therefore, useless. Ladies who ride astride get such bad falls that they soon give up this practice.

—JAMES FILLIS, *BREAKING AND RIDING* (1890)

Those who claim it is "unethical" to ask a horse to do something it would not do of its own inclination are being naïve and foolish; but equally naïve and foolish are those who expect to teach a horse to do their bidding without taking into account its natural inclinations.

—STEPHEN BUDIANSKY, *THE NATURE OF HORSES*

Whatever your purpose in riding, be sure that it includes the elements of fun and appreciation of your horse. Then you will be well on your way to becoming a true horseman.

—SHEILA WALL HUNDT, *INVITATION TO RIDING*

Many riding accidents would never have happened if people could control the false pride that makes them almost ashamed to ask for a quiet horse. But a good horseman can get anything he wants out of any horse, and I have never been able to figure out the illogic that makes poor riders think that they can control a high-spirited horse when, by their own admission, they can't even make the quiet horse move forward!

—GORDON WRIGHT, *LEARNING TO RIDE, HUNT, AND SHOW*

One of the most interesting and spectacular devices of the old farm horsemen was the stopping of a horse dramatically so that it would not move. That was called in East Anglia *jading* a horse; and it was from the practice more than any other that the horsemen sometimes earned the name of *horse-witches* because they were able to make the horse stand as though it were paralyzed or bewitched.

—ANTHONY DENT, *THE HORSE THROUGH FIFTY CENTURIES OF CIVILIZATION*

When the rider is thrown or is unable to make his mount do what he wants, it is always the horse that is blamed. When a horseman takes a spill, he looks to himself for the cause.

—Margaret Cabell Self, "Horseman (versus Rider)," *The Horseman's Encyclopedia*

———•••———

In contrast to the various sports which cultivate brute strength above all, riding preserves during the physical development a precise balance between strength and suppleness. This special quality, which naturally involves moral values too, leads to more balanced and disciplined training. Thus riding—the complete sport *par excellence*—tempers the body as it does the spirit.

—Commandant Jean Licart, *Start Riding Right*

There is much to be learned about balance and collection from observing a fine harness class. Many will ask, What has this to do with equitation? Why look at an event that has no rider? I do not believe there is a better place to learn how to handle a horse's mouth than in harness.

—HELEN CRABTREE, *SADDLE SEAT EQUITATION*

Women who have had the same opportunities as men of learning to ride, ride quite as well as they. But as a rule they do not *get* the chance of excelling, not are they "set right" by unpalatable home truths being told them without favour or affection.

—ALICE HAYES, *THE HORSEWOMAN*

To practice equestrian art is to establish a conversation on a higher level with the horse; a dialogue of courtesy and finesse.

—Nuno Oliveira, *Reflections on Equestrian Art*

If the rider's heart is in the right place, his seat will be independent of his hands.

—Piero Santini, *The Forward Impulse*

I've found that my most successful horses . . . all have certain traits in common. They're all very brave, good movers and solid individuals jumping, with the boldness to attack the cross-country courses. All of these horses in their own way are a bit difficult and are not to be ridden by a beginner. They're like John McEnroe of tennis: while they may be difficult, this strong character is what it takes to be an event horse.

—MIKE HUBER, "GETTING STARTED IN EVENTING,"
IN *RIDING FOR AMERICA*, EDITED BY NANCY JAFFER

Equestrian art, however, is something else which involves complete harmony between horse and rider, and that makes the rider feel that there have been moments of beauty and greatness which make a flight possible from all that is ordinary and mediocre.

—NUNO OLIVEIRA, *NOTES AND REMINISCENCES OF A PORTUGUESE RIDER*

I can tell you what judges like. They like a well-turned-out rider, smart as a whip, riding every ounce of his horse and looking as though he was glad to be in the ring.

—HELEN CRABTREE, *SADDLE SEAT EQUITATION*

A few years ago, I gave an interview in which I referred to sport as a crucible. My point was that if things are done correctly, the heat and pressure generated within the crucible of competition should burn away all that is base and false, leaving only the pure and true.

—JAMES C. WOFFORD, "THREE DAY RIDING AND TRADITIONS," IN *RIDING FOR AMERICA*, EDITED BY NANCY JAFFER

You cannot train a horse with shouts and expect it to obey a whisper.

—DAGOBERT D. RUNES, *LETTERS TO MY SON*

Eventing has been called the ultimate equestrian challenge, and not without reason. The event horse is the embodiment of courage, speed, dexterity, power, scope, precision, durability and a resolute will to prevail. The event rider, while possessing similar virtues in plentiful measure, must be able to elicit from a horse, within prudent limits, the willingness to deliver its talents on request, no matter how challenging the obstacle or how taxing the pace.

—GARY J. BENSON, WITH PHIL MAGGITTI, *IN THE IRONS*

. . . One of the most widely quoted of all riding axioms [is] Gustav Steinbrecht's "Ride your horse forward and hold it straight." Yet this trenchant advice of the great German horseman and writer is deceptive because it seems so simple, and so easy to put into practice; but those who have begun to really explore its richness of allusion will usually follow the quotation with "yes, that is the difficult thing." By the time the serious rider has learned why this is true, he will also know what riding in its best sense is all about.

—WILLIAM STEINKRAUS, *RIDING AND JUMPING*

For some people, working with the horse is just a way of stroking their own egos. Sometimes they have a lot of emotional baggage. Sometimes they lack awareness of their surroundings. That's why horses have so many problems with humans.

—TRAINER BOB BRANNAMAN [ONE OF THE INSPIRATIONS FOR *THE HORSE WHISPERER*], QUOTED IN *SMITHSONIAN* MAGAZINE

My first school horse was Pluto Kerka, who reminded me immediately and unmistakably that the reins were for the horse to be guided and not for the rider to hold on to. When my contact grew too strong, he leaned on the rein with all his weight or he rushed off. He could not have demonstrated more clearly how important it is to have to have an independent seat.

—ALOIS PODHAJSKY, *My Horses, My Teachers*

Learning about our horses is learning about ourselves as well, seeing how our personalities mesh or clash with the horses we choose to ride or train.

—LINDA TELLINGTON-JONES, *Getting in Ttouch:*
Understand and Influence Your Horse's Personality

A rider's total belief in an instructor is, of course, another essential. When students doubt me a little, I suggest other teachers they should go to. Without belief, discipline is a mockery, if not downright impossible.

—GEORGE H. MORRIS, *GEORGE H. MORRIS TEACHES BEGINNNERS TO RIDE*

—◆◆◆◆—

Everyone who wants justly to call himself—or herself—a rider should ponder the following statement very seriously: 99 per cent of all horses have quite a number of bad habits which are commonly put down to disobedience. And 99 per cent of all riders do not understand how to break their horses of such habits.

—WILHELM MÜSLER, *RIDING LOGIC*

A real horseman must not only be an expert—he must also be able to think and feel like a horse, that is, to realize that a horse is not equipped with *human* understanding. Such a horseman should be both horse and man—a centaur, not only physically, but also psychologically—anthropomorphic and hippomorphic.

—WALDEMAR SEUNIG, *HORSEMANSHIP*

———●•••●———

The noblest task of the riding teacher is to form the mind of the student as well, so that the latter comes to depend on the teacher less and less.

—WALDEMAR SEUNIG, *HORSEMANSHIP*

Indeed, if you get stuck on a particular problem, try asking all the good riders you know how they do it, and consult a good cross section of the serious books in your library . . . You may well get some fresh insights and at the very least, should get a consensus of conventional solutions, which can be quite helpful.

—William Steinkraus, *Reflections on Riding and Jumping*

The right way to do almost anything with horses is mainly a matter of using your natural intelligence in an uncomplicated manner, and this holds true also for the rider's basic mounted position. Simplicity and economy of movement are the goals of classical technique; the position of the rider upon the horse is the first fundamental.

—George H. Morris, *Hunter Seat Equitation*

The quality of the jump is determined by the quality of the approach to the fence, which is itself determined by the quality of the getaway from the previous fence and the turns between the the two jumps.

—MARY WANLESS, *THE NATURAL RIDER*

When your horse has reached his potential, leave it. It's such a nice feeling when you and your horses are still friends.

—DR. REINER KLIMKE, OLYMPIC DRESSAGE GOLD MEDALIST FOR GERMANY, QUOTED IN *HORSEPLAY* MAGAZINE

We follow the book. If we have disagreement, we open the book . . . We have nothing to invent. Everything in this sport has been written down already.

—NELSON PESSOA, QUOTED IN *HORSEPLAY* MAGAZINE

A good head means a pretty head and nothing more. Of course, vital functions go on inside of it. Eating, drinking, breathing, seeing, hearing and housing of the brain are life-and-death responsibilities. But structure, in this case, does not reflect usefulness.

—ALEXANDER MACKAY-SMITH, "CONFORMATION IN ACTION," IN *PRACTICAL HORSEMAN'S BOOK OF HORSEKEEPING*, EDITED BY M. A. STONERIDGE

The most important principle is to want to do it, to be committed before you start off to getting to the other side of every fence every time . . . If you are not certain about whether you want to go or not, do yourself and your horse a favor—don't start.

—CAPT. MARK PHILLIPS, *THE HORSE AND HOUND BOOK OF EVENTING*

I have often thought that "pride goeth before a fall" must have been written expressly for those riders who are too proud to reach for the mane, or to get their hands up before a jump, but not too proud to come back on their horse's mouth in mid-air, ruin a horse's mouth and disposition, and finally, run the risk of falling off.

—GORDON WRIGHT, *LEARNING TO RIDE, HUNT, AND SHOW*

The switch is rarely used as a means of punishment, though it has manifold uses as an aid. It is more often an ornament than a necessity. If you choose to depend upon it in the training of the horse, your understanding may be said to be as ephemeral as the swish of the switch itself.

—WILLIAM CAVENDISH, DUKE OF NEWCASTLE, *A GENERAL SYSTEM OF HORSEMANSHIP IN ALL ITS BRANCHES* (1658)

If I had to pick one thing that I had to hang my hat on, I would want the horse I was going to buy to have a face that I would enjoy seeing poked over the stall webbing every morning, waiting for breakfast.

—JAMES C. WOFFORD, *TRAINING THE THREE-DAY EVENT HORSE AND RIDER*

———

It cannot be too strongly impressed upon riding teachers that in every riding-school where ladies are to be taught, there should be at least one lady assistant. A gentleman can give all of the necessary instructions about the management of the horse and the handling of the reins better than most ladies; but in giving the idea of a correct seat and the proper disposal of the limbs, the presence of a lady instructor becomes necessary; in these matters she can instruct her own sex much better than a man can.

—ELIZABETH KARR, *THE AMERICAN HORSEWOMAN* (1884)

The riding hall is flooded with light. To the music of Bizet's "L'Arlesienne" suite, eight riders in brown dress-coats, riding white stallions with gold bridles, enter through the wide door. They solemnly lift their bicorne hats in salute to the portrait of the founder of the School, Emperor Charles VI, and doubtless also to its architect, Joseph Emanuel Fischer von Erlach, creator of the most beautiful manege in the world. The climax of the performance has been reached; the school quadrille begins.

—HANS HANDLER, *THE SPANISH RIDING SCHOOL*

Perfect harmony between the rider and his horse, i.e. beauty, is the ultimate goal of all dressage. The horse must be visibly at ease, and nothing in the rider's demeanor should betray how hard the road is.

—WILHELM MÜSLER, *RIDING LOGIC*

Nanticoke [a show jumper of the 1960s] reinforced a lesson I'd already started to learn from other horses: never try to muscle your way with a horse. There may or may not be an ideal way to do things; but in the horse world you have to be realistic, willing to try different solutions to a problem until you find one that works both for you and the horse. Letting Nanticoke jog along while I mounted wasn't ideal, but it was good horsemanship because we started the ride relaxed instead of with a fight.

—GRAND PRIX RIDER AND TRAINER RODNEY JENKINS, IN *PRACTICAL HORSEMAN'S BOOK OF RIDING, TRAINING, & SHOWING HUNTERS & JUMPERS*, EDITED BY M. A. STONERIDGE

As far as I'm concerned, a rider's fear is *real*—it's a non-negotiable issue. What feels like to her is what it is. Period. It doesn't matter whether her trainer, buddy, college professor, mother, or grandfather thinks she is overreacting, overprotective, or overindulgent.

—JANET SASSON EDGETTE, PSY.D., *HEADS UP! PRACTICAL SPORTS PSYCHOLOGY FOR RIDERS, THEIR FAMILIES AND THEIR TRAINERS*

Man has always attempted to become one with his horse when in the saddle, and he constantly seeks moments of perfect mutuality of movement, moments in which the skill becomes an art—if only for the duration of a heartbeat.

—HANS-HEINRICH ISENBART, *THE BEAUTY OF THE HORSE*

As riders, our problem is that too often we try to provide all the upward activity ourselves instead of allowing our bodies to use the bounce provided by the ground. You can become aware of this upward energy. You cannot hold it in reserve; if you do, you'll lose it . . . Center yourself and become aware of this energy as you ride.

—SALLY SWIFT, *CENTERED RIDING*

Talk to a dreamer and get caught up in the excitement. Sit on a fabulous horse and dream about having a horse of such quality to ride. Go to the big shows. Watch the great riders and dare to think . . . That could be me

—JANE SAVOIE, *THAT WINNING FEELING! A NEW APPROACH TO RIDING USING PSYCHOCYBERNETICS*

———◆•••◆———

After chefs, farriers are often reputed to be some of the most demanding prima donnas in existence. Whether they really are, or whether we—their clients—drive them to distraction is another matter: but the difference between throwing together a meal and creating a gourmet feast is not so unlike the difference between throwing on a set of shoes and practicing farriery as a precision art.

—MARY WANLESS, *FOR THE GOOD OF THE HORSE*

The rider, being the senior partner, has to make all efforts to learn the language of the horse, and to speak to him by means of that dialect.

—LT. COL. A. L. D'ENDRODY, *GIVE YOUR HORSE A CHANCE*

I have watched the [dressage] masters and they all seem to have a sort of Buddhistic detachment, an intense concentration on things like walking in a straight line, endlessly playing with the horse's mouth until he gives just as he should or monotonously starting and stopping *exactly* at X until the watcher is bored to death. Dressage's magic formula is the overpowering force of a combination of gentleness and repetition.

—PRINCESS PATRICIA GALVIN DE LA TOUR D'AUVERGNE, "DRESSAGE FOR GIRLS AND GRANDMOTHERS," IN *THE U.S. EQUESTRIAN TEAM BOOK OF RIDING*, EDITED BY WILLIAM STEINKRAUS

Prejudice is ugly in any form. There is not one breed of horse that is better than all others, or one best breed. Each has been bred for specific characteristics. A Paso Fino is not bred to pull a heavy wagon, few draft horses compete in calf roping, and a Quarter Horse is not designed to run a hundred-mile race. But there are more differences within a breed, than between breeds.

—JOHN LYONS, WITH SINCLAIR BROWN, *LYONS ON HORSES*

Show jumping . . . forms a partnership consisting of two performers who metamorphose into one: knowledge and intuition on behalf of the rider, together with a willingness on behalf of the horse. A willingness that has emerged out of a mutual understanding and trust.

—ELIZABETH FURST, *VISIONS OF SHOW JUMPING*

So much can be learned from watching others—sometimes just by understanding a feeling, rather than stiffly trying to do what you're told, without even realizing why you should do it. So many of our younger riders, even the top ones, work hours to put a horse in a "frame" only because their trainers tell them that it looks better or that the judge likes it. The hardest thing to get in riding is feeling, but that's what riding is all about. After a certain point, our sport really is 90 percent horse and how you can learn to adapt to that horse.

—OLYMPIC SHOW-JUMPING RIDER NORMAN DELLO JOIO, "LOVE CONQUERS ALL," IN *RIDING FOR AMERICA*, EDITED BY NANCY JAFFER

And their [horses'] mouths are very clever, so clever with the matter of locks on gates that it is the rare horseman who has had no occasion to be grateful that we have ten fingers and they only one mouth.

—VICKI HERNE, *ADAM'S TASK*

Riding allows me to distance myself from life's daily occurrences. When I am on a horse I forget everything else. I am absorbed by what I do. It is a certain escapism. When sitting on a horse my mind reaches a higher plane, especially when walking on a loose rein!

—Jean-Louis Guntz, quoted in *Visions of Dressage* by Elizabeth Furth

When a man is once well run away with, the first thing that occurs to him, I imagine, is how to stop his horse; but men by no means agree in the modes of bringing this matter about.

—Geoffrey Gambado, *An Academy for Grown Horsemen*

Mane, forelock, and tail are triple gifts bestowed by the gods upon the horse for the sake of pride and ornament, and here is the proof: a brood mare, so long as her mane is long and flowing, will not readily suffer herself to be covered by an ass; hence breeders of mules take care to clip the mane of the mare with a view to covering.

—XENOPHON, *ON HORSEMANSHIP*

———◆·◆·◆———

The wise horseman studies all he can regarding different methods of training, teaching, and riding, provided they are in accord with the fundamental principles followed by all good horsemen. Then he applies them according to the type of horse he is riding and the circumstances.

—MARGARET CABELL SELF, *RIDING WITH MARILES*

The best mouth is when the horse, without weighing on or fighting the hand, is firm, light and tempered on the bit. These three qualities go to make the perfectly-mouthed horse, and correspond to those of the rider's hand, which must be light, soft and firm.

—FRANÇOIS ROBICHON DE LA GUERINIERE, *ECOLE DE CAVALRIE*

———

There are few gentlemen, who, having moved much in society, have not at some time been called on to assist a lady into her saddle; and I know nothing so mortifying to a gentleman as to stand by.

—JOHN BUTLER, *THE HORSE AND HOW TO RIDE HIM*

There is a secret pleasing and cherishing of the horse with the bridle, which the rider must accomplish with so unperceiving a motion that none but the beast may know it.

—GERVASE MARKHAM, *THE COMPLEAT HORSEMAN*

A horsewoman should have great pliability of body, which she would acquire by practice in riding and other preliminary exercises, of which dancing is the best.

—JAMES FILLIS, *BREAKING AND RIDING*

There is no instant dressage. One should count in years, not in days.

—BENGT LJUNGQUIST, *PRACTICAL DRESSAGE MANUAL*

The educated horse is a thinking horse, and it seems that he understands that every now and then something happens that he must chalk up as a mistake and be done with it.

—GRAND PRIX SHOW-JUMPING RIDER AND TRAINER
DENNIS MURPHY, IN *PRACTICAL HORSEMAN*

There are a million miles of difference between the words "win" and "beat." We don't even allow the word "beat" on this farm. Because when you start talking about beating someone, you've lost your concentration. You're thinking about the opposition.

—SADDLE-SEAT TRAINER HELEN CRABTREE,
IN *CLASSIC* MAGAZINE

When in doubt, ride with your instincts.

—PAMELA C. BIDDLE AND JOEL E. FISHMAN,
ALL I NEED TO KNOW I LEARNED FROM MY HORSE

Be considerate of your horse. He is not a machine—and even machines run better with good driving.

—SHEILA WALL HUNDT, *INVITATION TO RIDING*

The worst fault a horse can exhibit in competition is the lack of honesty, for just as this is a major character flaw in a human, so it is in a horse.

—ANNA-JANE WHITE-MULLINS, *JUDGING HUNTERS AND HUNTER-SEAT EQUITATION*

The secrets of successful training are to work out what you want the horse to do and to explain to him in a way that he can understand; as a successful trainer of novice show jumpers once said, "training is just a series of repeated aids."

—CAROLYN HENDERSON AND LYNN RUSSELL, *BREAKING AND SCHOOLING*

"Tricks" have no place in the art of riding, since in moments of crisis, when effective action is most needed, the superficial "trick" never succeeds.

—Lt. Col. A. L. d'Endrody, *Give Your Horse a Chance*

You could put wings on some horses and not get them over [fences], they need to have heart.

—SHOW-JUMPING SUPERSTAR RIDER RODNEY JENKINS,
QUOTED IN *CLEAR ROUND* BY JULIA LONGLAND

For me, it is no good doing a lot of talking, or asking endless advice. I have to school myself to tackle it alone because when it comes to it, in the ring, you and the horse are out there on your own, and *you* have to make the decisions, be wrapped up in what you're doing.

—BRITISH SHOW-JUMPING RIDER GRAHAM FLETCHER, QUOTED IN *CLEAR ROUND* BY JULIA LONGLAND

Two words not commonly related to winning or losing at the horse show ring correlate to the color of the ribbons received. The two words are "act" and "react." Winners act. Nonwinners react.

—DON BURT, *WINNING WITH THE AMERICAN QUARTER HORSE*

But whether you regard the horse with awe or love, it is impossible to escape the sheer power of his presence, the phenomenal influence he exerts on the lives of all of us who decided at some stage that we wanted to become riders.

—MARY WANLESS, *THE NATURAL RIDER*

Bounce Once If You Believe In Diagonals.

—SUGGESTION FOR BUMPER STICKER

It is the very difficult horses that have the most to give you.

—LENDON GRAY

Horses are as much athletes as gymnasts, ballet dancers, or ice skaters, and unless they learn how to understand and use their bodies by "basic training," they can't be expected to perform well when the going gets tough.

—JOY SLATER, WITH STEVEN D. PRICE, *RIDING'S A JOY*

The aim of this noble and useful art [dressage] is solely to make horses supple, relaxed, flexible, compliant and obedient . . . without all of which a horse—whether he be meant for military service, hunting or dressage—will be neither comfortable in his movements nor pleasurable to ride.

—FRANÇOIS ROBICHON DE LA GUERINIERE, *ECOLE DE CAVALRIE* (1729)

No time spent in the saddle is wasted; as you learn to communicate with the horse and appreciate what he can do for you, it will add a fascinating dimension to your life.

—MARY GORDON-WATSON, *THE HANDBOOK OF RIDING*

The left side is the right side, and the right side is the wrong side.

—MAXIM ABOUT WHERE TO MOUNT AND DISMOUNT

Over, under or through.

—THREE-DAY EVENTING EXHORTATION ON HOW TO GET TO THE OTHER SIDE OF A CROSS-COUNTRY OBSTACLE

Consequently, the well-trained dressage horse should perform the natural paces with perfection. Any defects in these movements cannot be made up for by some other spectacular exercises. Riders or judges who allow themselves to be dazzled by such striking movements betray the true art of riding.

—ALOIS PODHAJSKY, *THE ART OF DRESSAGE*

All King Edward's Horses Canter Many Big Fences.

—MNEMONIC FOR THE A-K-E-H-C-M-B-F LETTERS AROUND A DRESSAGE ARENA

Furthermore, in a successful partnership, the rider has to know when he has to back off. He has to realize to what degree he can tolerate a horse's idiosyncrasies. He has to have a feeling for when he should enforce his own style onto the horse and when he has to accept the horse's.

—ELIZABETH FURST, *VISIONS OF SHOW JUMPING*

Ride your horse as you feel him, provided you were born to, or over the years have learned to feel! It is the one thing no book can teach you, no teacher can give you, the one conquest of the laurels which will be entirely yours.

—JEAN FROISSARD, *CLASSICAL HORSEMANSHIP FOR OUR TIME*

Had I but known about breathing in my youth, how much simpler my competitive riding life would have been.

—VICTOR HUGO-VIDAL, IN *SHOWING FOR BEGINNERS* BY HALLIE I. MCEVOY

A schooled horse is the best teacher, and a young horse should be ridden by an experienced rider.

—*THE PRINCIPLES OF RIDING* BY THE GERMAN NATIONAL EQUESTRIAN FEDERATION

A horseman is one who not only rides (although some fine horsemen do not ride at all) but also seeks to *know* the horse—its nature, needs and management—and feels a deep responsibility for his horses, the care they get, and the life they lead.

—SUSAN HARRIS, IN GEORGE H. MORRIS,
THE AMERICAN JUMPING STYLE

Natural talent, no matter how great, can't make up for a lack of basic knowledge and skills—but solid basics, combined with real desire and commitment, can make any rider a good rider.

—ANNE KURSINSKI, WITH MIRANDA LORRAINE, *ANNE KURSINSKI'S RIDING AND JUMPING CLINIC*

Horses will always be stronger than humans, but luckily we have a slight edge in the brains department, and through centuries of trial and error we have developed a number of effective ways of getting horses to do what we want.

—BARBARA BURN, *THE HORSELESS RIDER*

When I grew up in the horse business, to have a horse show we simply found an empty lot, put four posts in the ground, ran a rope around and called it a horse show arena.

—DON BURT, *WINNING WITH ARABIAN HORSES*

A rider has to be able to judge whether a horse is physically and mentally strong enough to carry out what has been asked for. In this way a horse will never get into a stressful situation. It is so important to ask oneself: "If the horse could talk and I was to ask it whether it actually knows what I want from it, would it reply, 'No idea!' or 'Yes, of course I do. I'm just not quite strong enough yet.'"

—ARTHUR KOTTAS-HELDENBERG, QUOTED IN, *VISIONS OF DRESSAGE* BY ELIZABETH FURST

———

What a horse does under compulsion he does blindly . . . The performances of horse or man so treated are displays of clumsy gestures rather than of grace and beauty. What we need is that the horse should of his own accord exhibit his finest airs and paces at set signals . . . Such are the horses on which gods and heroes ride.

—XENOPHON, *ON HORSEMANSHIP*

Not every rider can be elegant on a horse. I never try to fool any of my students. I explain to them that while they may ride as well as another person, they lack the natural elegance and poise of that person and, as a result, may be beaten by him. I want my students to know their limitations.

—TRAINER AND RIDER JIMMY WILLIAMS, IN *PRACTICAL HORSEMAN'S BOOK OF RIDING, TRAINING, & SHOWING HUNTERS & JUMPERS*, EDITED BY M. A. STONERIDGE

Fear almost always arises—in horses as well as in people—from concern about what might happen, and much more rarely from what *is* happening.

—MARY WANLESS, *FOR THE GOOD OF THE HORSE*

I myself have seen that when the Lipizzaner stallions gave a display within a horse show they did not pay the slightest attention to any of the other horses around them or to the bustle of the show, but stared intently in the direction where their comrades performed. It made me think of a theatre where some actors remain hidden in the wings to watch the stars of the group.

—ALOIS PODHAJSKY, *MY HORSES, MY TEACHERS*

———•••———

You know, you didn't get into riding because you were looking for more stress in your life. If you're not enjoying what you're doing, that's your cue to make a change. Don't wait for it to get better; *do* something to make it better. It's so important that you do whatever you can to preserve the sentiment that drew you into riding in the first place.

—JANET SASSON EDGETTE, PSY.D., *HEADS UP! PRACTICAL SPORTS PSYCHOLOGY FOR RIDERS, THEIR FAMILIES AND THEIR TRAINERS*

Can take a joke.

—HUNTER/JUMPER EXPRESSION USED TO DESCRIBE A HORSE THAT WILL PUT UP WITH BAD RIDES, ESPECIALLY BEING PUT TO BAD TAKE-OFF SPOTS IN FRONT OF FENCES [CONVERSELY, HORSES THAT WON'T TOLERATE SUCH BAD RIDES "CAN'T TAKE A JOKE"]

The riding of young horses is an excellent nerve tonic.

—GEOFFREY BROOKE, *TRAINING YOUNG HORSES TO JUMP*

Keep one leg on one side, the other leg on the other side, and your mind in the middle.

—HENRY TAYLOR

Experienced riders are not prone to brag. And usually newcomers, if they start out being boastful, end up modest.

—C. J. J. MULLEN

A perfect book on riding could be written only by a horse.

—VLADIMIR S. LITTAUER

3

Out of the West

A cowboy is a man with guts and a horse.

—ATTRIBUTED TO WILL JAMES

A man who rode good horses was usually a good man.

—WESTERN EXPRESSION, QUOTED IN *THEY RODE GOOD HORSES* BY DON HEDGPETH

He was a picture to make any cowboy miss a few heartbeats as he sometimes raced across the prairie sod and with head and tail up showed off the qualities that stuck out at his every move.

—WILL JAMES, *SMOKY THE COWHORSE*

Life is a catch pen full of rodeo broncs, and the way I figure it, forty-six years into this buck-out, the mission is to decide early on, *Did you come to hide, or did you come to ride?*

—PAUL ZARZYSKI, "GOOD HORSEKEEPING," IN *HORSE PEOPLE*, EDITED BY MICHAEL J. ROSEN

Oh, a ten dollar horse and a forty dollar saddle
I'm gonna quit punching Texas cattle.

—"THE CHISHOLM TRAIL"

He's cow-smart and brave—though sometimes a clown—and to the man with sky in his eye and mud on his boots the Quarter Horse is a faithful hand . . .
And a friend!

—REX CAUBLE, "WHAT IS A QUARTER HORSE," QUOTED IN *THE COMPLETE BOOK OF THE AMERICAN QUARTER HORSE* BY NELSON C. NYE

Any farmer can rope, but it takes a real cowboy to pull his slack.

—JACK KYLE

Riggin' ain't ridin'.

—WESTERN SAYING

There's a variety of horse minds as big as there is among human minds. Some need more pursuading than others, and a few of 'em, no matter how firm they're handled, will have to be showed again and again that they can't get away with this or that.

—WILL JAMES, *SMOKY THE COWHORSE*

Oh, when I die, take my saddle from the wall,
Put it on my pony, lead him out of his stall;
Tie my bones to his back, turn our faces to the West,
And we'll ride the prairies that we love best.

—"I RIDE AN OLD PAINT"

Greek mythology records the epic exploits of a wonderful winged horse named Pegasus. The stories of early Texas cow country speak of another legendary horse. He was called Steel Dust, and like Pegasus, he could fly, but without ever leaving the ground.

—DON HEDGPETH, THEY RODE GOOD HORSES: THE FIRST FIFTY YEARS OF THE AMERICAN QUARTER HORSE ASSOCIATION

When the stranger hit the saddle, Dunny quit the earth,
And travelled right straight up for all that he was worth,
A-pitching and a-squeeling and a-having wall-eye fits,
His hind feet perpendicular, his front feet in the bits.

—"ZEBRA DUN"

There never was a horse that couldn't be rode.
There never was a cowboy that couldn't be throwed.

—COWBOY SAYING

In the language of the range, to say that somebody is "as smart as a cutting horse" is to say that he is smarter than a Philadelphia lawyer, smarter than a steel trap, smarter than a coyote, smarter than a Harvard graduate—all combined. There just can't be anything smarter than a smart cutting horse. He can do everything but talk Meskin—and he understands that . . .

—JOE M. EVANS, *A CORRAL FULL OF STORIES*

In the Old West the phrase "left afoot" meant nothing short of being left flat on your back. "A man on foot is no man at all," the saying went. If an enemy could not take a man's life, the next best thing was to take his horse.

—J. FRANK DOBIE, *GUIDE TO LIFE AND LITERATURE OF THE SOUTHWEST*

Wrangle was one of the horses that left his viciousness in the home corral. What he wanted was to be free of mules and burros and steers, to roll in dust-patches, and then to run down the wide, open, windy sage-plains, and at night browse and sleep in the cool wet grass of a springhole. Jerd knew the sorrel when he said of him, "Wait till he smells the sage!"

—ZANE GREY, *RIDERS OF THE PURPLE SAGE*

Rodeoing is about the only sport you can't fix. You'd have to talk to the bulls and horses, and they wouldn't understand you.

—BILL LINDERMAN

A cowboy climbed aboard a bronc, which commenced to buck. The bronc threw one particular buck that caused the cowboy to lose his stirrups while, at the same time, the bronc caught a hind leg in one of the stirrups. Whereupon the cowboy went flying out of the saddle.

When the onlookers asked the cowboy what had happened, he replied, "well, boys, when I looked down and saw that bronc's foot in the stirrup, I said to myself, "hell, if he's gettin' on, I'd better get off."

—ANONYMOUS

When you're young and you fall off a horse, you may break something. When you're my age and you fall off, you splatter.

—ROY ROGERS

Never approach a bull from the front, a horse from the rear or a fool from any direction.

—COWBOY SAYING

———•••••———

The pony saw through it. No feint hoodwinked him. This animal was thoroughly a man of the world. His undistracted eye stayed fixed upon the dissembling foe, and the gravity of his horse-expression made the matter one of high comedy. Then the rope would sail out at him, but he was already elsewhere; and if horses laugh, gayety must have abounded in that corral.

—OWEN WISTER, *THE WESTERNER*

May your belly never grumble,
May your heart never ache.
May your horse never stumble,
May your cinch never break.

—COWBOY BLESSING

Their horses appear to be of an excellent race; they are lofty, eligantly *[sic]* formed, active and durable . . . Some of these horses are pied with large spots of white irregularly scattered and intermixed with a black, brown, bay or some other dark color.

—MERIWETHER LEWIS COMMENTING ON APPALOOSA HORSES OWNED BY THE NEZ PERCE, QUOTED IN *THE HORSE IN THE WEST* BY BRADLEY SMITH

A good horse is never a bad color.

—COWBOY SAYING

Practice sharpens, but overschooling blunts the edge. If your horse isn't doing right, the first place to look is yourself.

—JOE HEIM, QUOTED IN *CUTTING, ONE RUN AT A TIME* BY BARBRA SCHULTE

———•◦•———

Men will keep going on their nerve or their head,
But you cannot ride a horse when he's dead.

—LEONARD BACON, "COLORADO MORTON'S RIDE"

When that horse hit the ground I felt as though Saint Peter and all the guards of the Pearly Gates who I'd been to see just a second before, had put their foot down on me and was trying to push me through the earth to the hot place. The saddle horn was tickling me under the chin and one of my feet touched the ground, my other one was alongside the horse's jaw.

—WILL JAMES, *THE DRIFTING COWBOY*

For prairie service, horses which have been raised exclusively upon grass and have never been fed upon grain, or *range horses* as they are called in the West, are decidedly the best, and will perform more hard labor than those that have been stabled and grained.

—CAPT. RANDOLPH B. MARCY, *THE PRAIRIE TRAVELER*

That's a horse to cross rivers on.

— WESTERN EXPRESSION DESCRIBING A GOOD SWIMMING HORSE

I want free life and I want fresh air;
And I sigh for the canter after the cattle,
The crack of the whips like shots in a battle,
The medley of horns and hooves and heads.

— FRANK DESPREZ, "LASCA"

Don't pitch your rope like you were through with it.

— ADVICE TO STEER AND CALF ROPERS, QUOTED BY THOMAS McGUANE, "ROPING A TO B," SOME HORSES

A cowman saddles and unsaddles his own horse, and an offer to help is unwelcome.

— RAMON ADAMS, THE COWMAN'S CODE OF ETHICS

High-powered saddles ain't half as hard to find as high-powered hombres in 'em.

—WESTERN SAYING

The toughest broncs is them you rode some other place.

—WESTERN SAYING

If you're a cowboy and you're dragging a guy behind your horse, I bet it would really make you mad if you looked back and the guy was reading a magazine.

—JACK HANDEY, *DEEP THOUGHTS*

No matter how hungry he may be, [the cowman] takes care of his horse before looking after his own comfort.

—RAMON ADAMS, *THE COWMAN'S CODE OF ETHICS*

A cutting competition is nothing more than a contest of "oh shits" and "attaboys." And the person with more attaboys is the winner.

—BUSTER WELCH, QUOTED IN *TRAINING AND SHOWING THE CUTTING HORSE* BY LYNN CAMPION

———

In those border days every rider loved his horse as a part of himself. If there was a difference between any rider of the sage and Bostil, it was, as Bostil had more horses, so had he more love.

—ZANE GREY, "THE HORSES OF BOSTIL'S FORD"

I once gave Eugen Herrigel's little masterpiece *Zen and the Art of Archery* to Buster [Welch, the cutting-horse trainer] to read and he concluded that its application to horsemanship was that if you are thinking about your riding, you are interfering with your horse.

—THOMAS MCGUANE, "BUSTER," *SOME HORSES*

Never forget that the basic principles of cutting are left-stop-right-stop. You've got a cow with no brains trying to get back to the herd, and all you have to do is stay even with her.

—CHUBBY TURNER, QUOTED IN *TRAINING AND SHOWING THE CUTTING HORSE* BY LYNN CAMPION

Halted in animated expectancy or running in abandoned freedom, the mustang was the most beautiful, the most spirited and the most inspiring creature ever to print foot on the grasses of America.

—J. Frank Dobie, *The Mustangs*

———

When I was doctor'n' a horse, the story would come up about what he had done and who he had saved and they'd say, "Save him if you can!" Nobody in the ranch country ever insulted a good horse by talking about what it would cost to replace him and the telephone operators whose help was indispensable in this particular epidemic were mostly all girls and women with ranch background or who were married to a cowboy and the general thought in treating horses was never about money but instead was to save the horse for the good he had done or for what he meant to somebody.

—Ben K. Green, *The Village Horse Doctor: West of the Pecos*

My foot's in the stirrup, my bridle's in my hand,
Good morning, young lady, my hoss he won't stand.

Old Paint's a good pony, he paces when he can,
Goodbye, ol' Paint, I'm leaving Cheyenne.

—"Goodbye Old Paint"

4

A Shakespearean Interlude

[Certainly the most widely known equestrian quotation in the English language comes from William Shakespeare's historical play *King Richard III*:]

A horse! A horse! My kingdom for a horse!

ACT V, SCENE 4

[However, the Bard's plays and poetry contain many more references to horses and horsemanship. Let's begin with this extended excerpt from *Venus and Adonis*:]

But lo! from forth a copse that neighbours by,
Abreeding jennet, lusty, young, and proud,
Adonis' tramping courier doth espy,
And forth she rushes, snorts and neighs aloud:
The strong-neck'd steed, being tied unto a tree,
Breaketh his rein, and to her straight goes he.

Imperiously he leaps, he neighs, he bounds,
And now his woven girths he breaks asunder;
The bearing earth with his hard hoof he wounds,
Whose hollow womb resounds like heaven's thunder;
The iron bit he crusheth 'tween his teeth,
Controlling what he was controlled with.

His ears up-prick'd; his braided hanging mane
Upon his compass'd crest now stand on end;
His nostrils drink the air, and forth again,
As from a furnace, vapours doth he send:
His eye, which scornfully glisters like fire,
Shows his hot courage and his high desire.

Sometime he trots, as if he told the steps,
With gentle majesty and modest pride;
Anon he rears upright, curvets and leaps,
As who should say, 'Lo! thus my strength is tried;
And this I do to captivate the eye
Of the fair breeder that is standing by.'

What recketh he his rider's angry stir,
His flattering 'Holla', or his 'Stand, I say'?
What cares he now for curb or pricking spur?
For rich caparisons or trapping gay?
He sees his love, and nothing else he sees,
Nor nothing else with his proud sight agrees.

Look, when a painter would surpass the life,
In limning out a well-proportion'd steed,
His art with nature's workmanship at strife,
As if the dead the living should exceed;
So did this horse excel a common one,
In shape, in courage, colour, pace and bone.

Round-hoof'd, short-jointed, fetlocks shag and long,
Broad breast, full eye, small head, and nostril wide,
High crest, short ears, straight legs and passing strong,
Thin mane, thick tail, broad buttock, tender hide:
Look, what a horse should have he did not lack,
Save a proud rider on so proud a back.

—*VENUS AND ADONIS*, LINES 259–300

[In the following exchange, Richard II, imprisoned after Henry
Bolingbroke usurped the throne, is told by a groom that
Brolingbroke rode the king's horse, Barbary, to Bolingbroke's
coronation as King Henry IV:]

King Richard: Rode he on Barbary? Tell me, gentle
    friend,
How went he under him?
Groom: So proudly as if he disdain'd the ground.
King Richard: So proud that Bolingbroke was on his
    back!
That jade hath eat bread from my royal hand;
This hand hath made him proud with clapping him.
Would he not stumble? Would he not fall down,
Since pride must have a fall, and break the neck
Of that proud man that did usurp his back?
Forgiveness, horse! Why do I rail on thee,
Since thou, created to be aw'd by man,
Wast born to bear? I was not made a horse;
And yet I bear a burden like an ass,
Spurr'd, gall'd and tir'd, by jaucing Bolingbroke.

—*KING RICHARD II*, ACT V, SCENE 5

But hollow men, like horses hot at hand,
Make gallent show and promise of their mettle;
But when they should endur the bloody spur,
They fall their crests, and like deceitful jades,
Sink in the trial.

—*Julius Caesar*, ACT IV, SCENE 2

———•••——

Young hot colts being raged do rage the more.

—*King Richard II*, ACT II, SCENE 1

———•••——

Like unback'd colts, they prick'd their ears,
Advanced their eyelids, lifted up their noses
As they smelled music.

—*The Tempest*, ACT IV, SCENE 1

I wish your horses swift and sure of foot;
And so I do command you to their backs.

—*MACBETH*, ACT III, SCENE 1

He doth nothing but talk of his horse.

—*THE MERCHANT OF VENICE*, ACT 1, SCENE 2

Let the galled jade wince, our withers are unrung.

—*HAMLET*, ACT III, SCENE 2

He grew unto his seat; And to such wonderous doing
    brought his horse,
As he had been incorpsed and demi-natured
With the brave beast.

—*HAMLET*, ACT IV, SCENE 7

Rise from the ground like feather'd Mercury,
And vaulted with such ease into his seat
As if an angel dropp'd down from the clouds,
And turn and wind a fiery Pegasus
And witch the world with noble horsemanship.

—*HENRY IV, PART ONE*, ACT IV, SCENE 1

I will not change my horse with any that treads on four pasterns. Ca ha! He bounds from the earth, as if his entrails were hairs, le cheval volant, the Pegasus, chez les narines de feu! When I bestride him, I soar, I am a hawk: he trots the air; the earth sings when he touches it; the basest horn of his hoof is more musical than the pipe of Hermes . . . he is pure air and fire . . . the prince of palfreys; his neigh is like the bidding of a monarch and his countenance enforces homage.

—*HENRY V*, ACT III, SCENE 7

Those that tame wild horses
Pace 'em not in their hands to make 'em gentle,
But strip their mouths with stubborn bits, and spur 'em
Till they obey the menage.

—*KING HENRY VIII*, ACT V, SCENE 3

I jest to Oberon, and make him smile
When I a fat and bean-fed horse beguile,
Neighing in likeness of a filly foal.

—*A MIDSUMMER NIGHT'S DREAM*, ACT II, SCENE 1

Her chariot is an empty hazel-nut
Made by the joiner squirrel or old grub,
Time out of mind the fairies' coachmakers.
And in this state she gallops night by night
Through lovers' brains, and then they dream of love.

—*ROMEO AND JULIET*, ACT I, SCENE 4

Gallop apace, you fiery-footed steeds,
Toward Phoebus' lodging.

—*Romeo and Juliet*, ACT III, SCENE 2

Beggers mounted run their horses to death.

—*Henry VI, Part Three*, ACT I, SCENE 4

[Similar to "Set a beggar on horseback and he will ride a gallop"
(Robert Burton, *Anatomy of Melancholy)* and the German proverb,
"Set a beggar on horseback, and he'll outride the Devil."]

Time travels in divers paces with divers persons. I'll tell
you who Time ambles withal, who Time trots withal,
who Time gallops withal, and who he stands still withal.

—*As You Like It*, ACT III, SCENE 2

He uses his folly like a stalking horse.

—*As You Like It* ACT V, SCENE 4

As two men ride of a horse, one must ride behind.

—*Much Ado about Nothing*, ACT III, SCENE 5

Well could he ride, and often men would say
"That horse his mettle from his rider takes:
Proud of subjection, noble by the sway,
What rounds, what bounds, what course, what stop he
　　makes!"
And controversy hence a question takes,
Whether the horse by him became his deed,
Or he his manage by the well-doing steed.

—*A Lover's Complaint*, LINES 106–112

What a piece of work is a horse! How noble in reason! How infinite in faculty! In form and moving how express and admirable! In action how like an angel! In apprehension how like a man! The beauty of the world! The paragon of animals!

—JAMES AGATE, *ALARUMS AND EXCURSIONS* [MODELED ON HAMLET'S "WHAT A PIECE OF WORK IS MAN!" SPEECH]

5

Racing—The Sport of Kings

[Neptune] created the horse and was the patron of horse races. His own horses had brazen hooves and golden manes.

—*Bulfinch's Mythology*, "Neptune"

The utter joy of riding Template lay in the immense power which he generated. There was no need to make the best of things, on his back; to fiddle and scramble, and to hope for others to blunder, and find nothing to spare for a finish. He had enough reserve strength for his jockey to be able to carve up the race as he wished, and there was nothing in racing, I thought, more ecstatic than that.

—*Dick Francis, Nerve*

[Sunday Silence, winner of the 1989 Kentucky Derby] seemed to be some kind of prehistoric throwback, a living legend of the days when horses were hunted, when fear and hunger ruled their lives. In a classy stable of calm, earnest animals, Sunday Silence was Al Capone singing in the Vienna Boys Choir.

—JAY HOVDEY, *WITTINGHAM, THE STORY OF A THOROUGHBRED LEGEND*

When you peel back the layers of racing, you are left with the horse and the groom.

—TRAINER AND TV COMMENTATOR CHARLSIE CANTY, QUOTED IN *THE BACKSTRETCH* MAGAZINE

Horse racing is the sport of kings and the trap of fools.

—ANONYMOUS

It is not best that we all think alike; it is difference of opinion that makes horse races.

—MARK TWAIN

———•••••———

Too much hope is perhaps the worst sin in horse racing.

—SIMON BARNES, "TALKING HORSES" IN THE *TIMES* (LONDON)

———•••••———

A horse gallops with his lungs, preserves with his heart, and wins with his character.

—FEDERICO TESIO, *BREEDING THE RACEHORSE*

———•••••———

The harrowing uncertainty of the turf.

—SPORTS COLUMNIST AND AUTHOR RED SMITH

As some swift horse
Is reined in by his rider, when he strains
Unto the race-course, and he neighs, and champs
The curbing bit, dashing his chest with foam,
And his feet eager for the course are still
Never, his restless hooves are clattering aye;
His mane is a stormy cloud, he tosses high
His head with snortings, and his lord is glad . . .

—QUINTUS SMYRNAEUS, "THE FALL OF TROY"

The race is not always to the swift nor the battle to the strong—but that's the way to bet.

—DAMON RUNYAN

Horses have never hurt anyone yet, except when they bet on them.

—STUART CLOETE

I'll be around as long as horses think I'm smarter than they are.

—TRAINER JAMES E. "SUNNY JIM" FITZSIMMONS [WHO CONTINUED TO TRAIN HORSES INTO HIS NINETIES]

Now a barrier looms, dark and menacing, in your path. You feel an almost imperceptible change in your horse's momentum as he adjusts his stride to meet the takeoff point. You tighten your legs against his sides to give encouragement in the last few critical strides. Your body picks up the horse's emphatic rhythm, and you feel the great hindquarters gather under you. Suddenly, you are in the air, feeling the clean, exhilarating sensation of a flight.

You are on a 'chaser.

—RAYMOND WOOLFE JR., *STEEPLECHASING*

Breed the best to the best, and hope for the best.

—TRADITIONAL BREEDING ADVICE

In a few generations you can breed a racehorse. The recipe for making a man like Delacroix is less well known.

—JEAN RENOIR, *RENOIR, MY FATHER*

Morning glory.

—RACETRACK EXPRESSION FOR A HORSE THAT TURNS IN IMPRESSIVE MORNING WORKOUTS, BUT FAILS TO WIN IN THE AFTERNOON

I hope I break even, I need the money.

—JOE E. LEWIS [ON BETTING]

You can eat your betting money, but never bet your eating money.

—SIGN IN MANY RACETRACK CAFETERIAS

A racehorse is an animal that can take several thousand people for a ride at the same time.

—ANONYMOUS

You can take an old mule and run him and feed him and train him and get him in the best shape of his life, but you ain't going to win the Kentucky Derby!

—PEPPER MARTIN

Ascot is so exclusive that it is the only racecourse in the world where the horses own the people.

—ART BUCHWALD

Eclipse first, the rest nowhere.

—CAPTAIN O'KELLEY, QUOTED IN *ANNALS OF SPORTING* [ECLIPSE WAS THE OUTSTANDING RACEHORSE OF EIGHTEENTH-CENTURY ENGLAND]

Everyone knows that horse racing is carried on mainly for the delight and profit of fools, ruffians, and thieves.

—GEORGE GISSING, *THE PRIVATE PAPERS OF HENRY RYECROFT*

And such running! It was rather the long leaping of lions in harness; but for the lumbering chariot, it seemed the four were flying.

—LEW WALLACE, *BEN-HUR*

The Perfect Horseman is quiet on a horse. The calmness which springs from confidence in his own ability extends to the horse and quietens him too. Nothing frightens a horse as much as a frightened rider, and nothing will make a horse more restless and fidgety than a rider who cannot sit still . . .

Everyone realizes that a bad rider can make a thoroughbred look like a cart-horse, but unless a horse is fleet of foot the Perfect Horseman and the Perfect Jockey rolled into one cannot win races on him. The jockey is there to guide, help, drive, cajole, or even hoax his horse into the winner's enclosure, but he cannot go faster than the horse.

—DICK FRANCIS, *THE SPORT OF QUEENS*

The profession of book writing makes horse racing seem like a solid, stable business.

—JOHN STEINBECK

If you've never been crazy about thoroughbreds it's because you've never been around where they are much and don't know any better. They're beautiful. There isn't anything so lovely and clean and full of spunk and honesty and everything as some racehorses.

—SHERWOOD ANDERSON, "I WANT TO KNOW WHY"

I was nuts about the horses, too. There's something about it, when they come out and go up the track to the post. Sort of dancy and tight looking with the jock keeping a tight hold on them and maybe easing off a little and letting them run a little going up.

—ERNEST HEMINGWAY, "MY OLD MAN"

The sunshine's golden gleam is thrown
On sorrel, chestnut, bay and roan;
The horses prance and paw and neigh,
Fillies and colts like kittens play,
And dance and toss their rippled manes
Shining and soft as silken skeins.

—OLIVER WENDELL HOLMES SR., "HOW THE OLD HORSE WON THE BET"

Betting the ponies is done in various methodical ways by professionals, haphazardly by some enthusiasts, and often in a rather bizarre fashion by others just out for a day's lark.

—COOKY MCCLUNG, *HORSEFOLK ARE DIFFERENT*

And it is marvelous to me
That grown-up gentlemen can be
So simple, so confiding;
I envy them, but, O my son,
I cannot think they have done
A great amount of riding.

—SIR A. P. HERBERT, "THE RACING-MAN"

A hoss is a gen'leman, kid. It hurts him to lose a race, it breaks him—permanent—to see a race.

—LINCOLN STEFFENS, *THE AUTOBIOGRAPHY OF LINCOLN STEFFENS*

But if we offer prizes for races with ridden horses—young and half-grown colts as well as full-grown beasts—we shall be cultivating a sport well in keeping with the nature of our territory.

—PLATO, *LAWS VIII*

Jimmy Shrewin was not one of those philosophers who justify the great and growing game of betting on the ground that it improves the breed of an animal less and less in use. He justified it much more simply—he lived by it.

—JOHN GALSWORTHY, *CARAVAN*

"Races are won with that seat, sir."

"Be damned to that," said my uncle Valentine. "If the horse is good enough, he'll win with the rider facing his tail."

—DOROTHEA DONN BYRNE, "DESTINY BAY"

The little bright mare, made of nerves and steel springs,
Shot level beside him, shot ahead as with wings.
Charles felt his horse quicken, felt the desperate beat
Of the blood in his body from his knees to his feet.

—JOHN MASEFIELD, "RIGHT ROYAL"

There are a hundred ways to lose a race, but only one way to win one.

—RACING MAXIM

Watch out for that first jump out of the [starting] gate— it's a big one!

—ADVICE TO NOVICE JOCKEYS

A racetrack is a place where the human race is secondary.

—ANONYMOUS

The riders in a race do not stop short when they reach the goal. There is a little finishing canter before they come to a standstill . . . The canter that brings you to a standstill need not be only coming to rest. It cannot be while you still live.

—SUPREME COURT JUSTICE OLIVER WENDELL HOLMES JR.,
REFLECTING ON RETIREMENT IN A RADIO ADDRESS ON HIS NINETIETH
BIRTHDAY

The more you know, the more you win. That is the allure of horse race handicapping.

—CHARLES CARROLL, *HANDICAPPING SPEED*

Losers walking around with money in their pockets are always dangerous, not to be trusted. Some horse always reaches out and grabs them.

—BILL BARICH, *LAUGHING IN THE HILLS*

Horse racing is animated roulette.

—ROGER KAHN, "INTELLECTUALS AND SCHOLARS," *THE AMERICAN SCHOLAR*

Most good horses know when they'd won: filled their lungs and raised their heads with pride. Some were definitely depressed when they lost. Guilt they never felt, nor shame nor regret nor compassion.

—DICK FRANCIS, *BREAK IN*

The sights and sounds of the countryside, as well as the color and action and excitement of the racecourse, are what turn me on: the mare suckling her foal, the renegade foal bothering all the others, the yearling who is boss of the field.

—THOROUGHBRED RACEHORSE OWNER AND BREEDER PAUL MELLON

Horse sense is the thing a horse has which keeps it from betting on people.

—W. C. FIELDS

⸺•⋅•⸺

If you start getting nervous about getting hurt you will be . . . If you are worrying about the danger it's time to give up.

—JASON WEAVER

⸺•⋅•⸺

Politics is like a racehorse. A good jockey must know how to fall with the least possible danger.

—EDOUARD HERRIOTT

According to the best traditions, sunrise on a spring morning is supposed to make a guy glad to be alive. But at sunrise, how can a guy tell he's alive? There is a law in the benighted state of New York which bars children from racetracks in the afternoon, the archaic theory being that frequenting a gambling hell is an occasion of sin for minors. Wherefore a small boy, if he is to be reared properly, must be taken to the track for the morning works.

—RED SMITH, "CLOCKERS ARE LITTLE MEN," IN *THE RED SMITH READER*

As I browse through my field in Virginia
And muse, at the close of the day
Once again they will give me a medal
Made of silver, although it ain't hay.

—PAUL MELLON, IMAGINING THE APPRECIATION OF ONE OF HIS HORSES THAT WON A PRIZE

Horses that are gray won't earn their hay.

—RACETRACK PREJUDICE

Here is living harmony in horseflesh; an embodiment of rhythm and modulation, of point and counterpoint, that sang to the eye and made music in the heart.

—JOHN HERVEY [SALVADORE] ON THE GREAT RACEHORSE EQUIPOISE

He was as near living flame as horses ever get.

—JOE PALMER ON MAN O'WAR

A dark horse which had never been thought of, and which the careless St. James had never observed in the list, rushed past the grandstand in sweeping triumph.

—BENJAMIN DISRAELI

Lead him away!—far down the past,
Where sentiment has fled;
But, gentlemen, just at last,
Drink deep!—the Thoroughbred!

—JOHN TAINTOR FOOTE, "THE THOROUGHBRED"

The heart is like a race horse on a plain, easy to let go,
hard to rein in.

—CHINESE PROVERB

The blood runs hot in the Thoroughbred and the
courage runs deep. In the best of them, pride is limitless.
This is their heritage and they carry it like a banner.
What they have, they use.

—C. W. ANDERSON

The fires burnt high in him. He should have lived with the wild horses of the prairie where he could have been boss. There the issue would have been settled quickly; he would have ruled or died. But civilization got him instead. Man laid hold of his bridle. 'All right,' said Display, 'you asked for it,' and he gave it to them. Finally he did what they asked but not because he had changed his mind.

—J. A. ESTES, ON THE THOROUGHBRED RACEHORSE DISPLAY

Don't ever call me a jockette.

—ROBYN SMITH, FEMALE JOCKEY

The blue ribbon of the turf.

—BENJAMIN DISRAELI, DESCRIBING THE ENGLISH DERBY RACE, IN *THE LIFE OF LORD GEORGE BENTINCK*

Horses and jockeys mature earlier than people—which is why horses are admitted to racetracks at the age of two, and jockeys before they are old enough to shave.

—DICK BEDDOES

Don't fall off.

—ADVICE GIVEN BY HOLLIE HUGHES, AN ELDERLY TRAINER, TO SECRETARIAT'S JOCKEY RON TURCOTTE BEFORE THE 1973 BELMONT STAKES (WHICH SECRETARIAT WENT ON TO WIN BY THIRTY-THREE LENGTHS)

If you could call the thing a horse. If it hadn't shown a flash of speed in the straight, it would have gotten mixed up with the next race.

—P. G. WODEHOUSE, *VERY GOOD, JEEVES*

I feel as a horse must feel when the beautiful cup is given to the jockey.

—EDGAR DEGAS, ON SEEING ONE OF HIS PAINTINGS SOLD AT AUCTION

Out on the Texas plains a fellow had to be a smart horseman to win a race and a smarter one to win a bet—and collect it!

—SAMUEL CLAY HILDRETH, *THE SPELL OF THE TURF*, QUOTED IN *THE COLONIAL QUARTER RACE HORSE* BY ALEXANDER MACKAY-SMITH

A word is enough for a wise man, and a flick of the whip for a fleet horse.

—CHINESE PROVERB

There appears to be no immunity to this dangerous germ. If as a parent you observe your little precious pick up a toy horse, make galloping noises, and plop it over a block, screaming "Win!" you've had it. The jumping rider's disease is loose in your house.

—RAYMOND WOOLFE JR., *STEEPLECHASING*

I bought five more horses [after John Henry, 1981 and 1984 Horse of the Year]. Two are with the Canadian mounted police. One's directing traffic out on Union Avenue. One is up at Cornell: they can't figure out if it's a male or female. And a last one a friend bought for $5,000 to spare me further embarassment.

—SAM RUBIN, QUOTED IN *THEY'RE OFF! HORSE RACING AT SARATOGA* BY EDWARD HOTALING

A trainer can always find an excuse for a defeat, whether it's a mistake in judgment by the jockey or the conditions of the track or a bit of poor racing luck. Maybe just a little adjustment—a new rider or a change in equipment or a different post position—will make the next outcome different. "This is the great thing about racing," trainer D. Wayne Lucas once said. "There's always another race."

—BILLY REED, *THOROUGHBRED: A CELEBRATION OF THE BREED*

6

A Pack of Hunting Quotations

I saw the hounds occasionally, sometimes pouring over a green bank, as the charging breaker lifts and flings itself, sometimes driving across a field, as the white tongues of foam slide racing over the sand; and always ahead of me was Flurry Knox, goes as a man goes who knows his country, who knows his horse, and whose heart is wholly and absolutely in the right place.

—E. O. SOMERVILLE AND MARTIN ROSS, *SOME EXPERIENCES OF AN IRISH R.M.*

It ain't the 'unting as 'urts 'un, it's the 'ammer, 'ammer, 'ammer along the 'ard, 'igh ground.

—*PUNCH* MAGAZINE CARTOON CAPTION

There are only two classes of good society in England; the equestrian classes and the neurotic classes. It isn't mere convention; everybody can see that the people who hunt are the right people and the people who don't are the wrong ones.

—GEORGE BERNARD SHAW, *HEARTBREAK HOUSE*

Old John had brought his Whips [Whippers-In], all five of them still mounted like himself and fresh from the hunt, clomping into the grand salon to admire Whistle-jacket, one of the finest portraits of a horse ever painted by George Stubbs. The horses of the five Whips trod on polished floors and French floor coverings, the men said down a man that looking at Whistlejacket from the saddle gave a new and admirable perspective to the grandeur of the horse, no matter that several of the living horses shied from the painted animal or attempted to rear up in imitation of it. This event sent Great-Grandmother to her bed for a week.

—JOHN HAWKES, *WHISTLEJACKET*

With the Meadowbrook Hunt they were always in
    front,
And fearless of all disaster.
Over bar and gate they would lead on straight.
Old Mohawk—and his Master.

—ANONYMOUS QUATRAIN IN HONOR OF ELLIOTT ROOSEVELT,
MASTER OF THE MEADOWBROOK HUNT ON LONG ISLAND, NEW
YORK, AND HIS HORSE, OLD MOHAWK [ROOSEVELT WAS THE
FATHER OF FIRST LADY ELEANOR ROOSEVELT]

Today, all day, I rode upon the down,
With hounds and horsemen, a brave company . . .
And once, when check'd, a thrush sang, and my horse
Prick'd his quick ears as to a sound unknown.
. . . Your face my quarry was. For it I rode,
My horse a thing of wings, myself a god.

—WILFRID SCAWEN BLUNT, "ST. VALENTINE'S DAY"

That foxhunting is not a competitive sport is a fact which should be known to all. Unfortunately, however, in the excitement of a fast hunt, it is frequently recognized by too few.

—MARJORIE B. MCDONALD, M.F.H., IN GORDON WRIGHT, *LEARNING TO RIDE, HUNT, AND SHOW*

'Aving the 'ead of a dutchess and the arse of a cook.

—ENGLISH DESCRIPTION OF AN IDEAL HUNTING HORSE

Do not approach the sport faint-heartedly or you will miss the uplift of spirit that it can provide. Those who must wait for perfect weather and footing seldom go out foxhunting.

—SHEILA WALL HUNDT, *INVITATION TO RIDING*

He all the country could outrun,
Could leave both man and horse behind;
And often, ere the chase was done,
He reeled, and was stone-blind.

—WILLIAM WORDSWORTH, "SIMON LEE, THE OLD HUNTSMAN"

Let your gelding be: if you check or chide
He stumbles at once and you're out of the hunt;
For three hundred gentlemen, able to ride,
On hunters accustomed to bear the brunt . . .

—JOHN DAVIDSON, "A RUNNABLE STAG"

The horses snort to be at the sport,
The dogs are running free;
The woods rejoice at the merry noise
Of hey taranta tee ree.

—WILLIAM GRAY, "THE KING'S HUNT IS UP"

It was said of Mr. Knox, private chaplain to the Duke of Rutland, that he wore boots and spurs under his cassock and surplice, and "thought of horses even in the pulpit." The Duke family could always tell by the speed of morning prayers if Mr. Knox were hunting that day or not.

—BARBARA TUCHMAN, *THE PROUD TOWER*

A jolly wight there was, that rode
Upon a sorry mare.

—THOMAS HOOD, "THE EPPING HUNT"

The first Marchioness [of Salisbury] was painted by Sir Joshua Reynolds, and hunted till the day she died at eighty-five, who, half-blind and strapped to the saddle, she was accompanied by a groom who would shout, when her horse approached a fence, "Jump, dammit, my Lady, jump!"

—BARBARA TUCHMAN, *THE PROUD TOWER*

Three jolly gentlemen
Dressed in red
Rode their horses
Up to bed.

—WALTER DE LA MARE, "THE HUNTSMEN"

Remember that the most important gait of the hunter is the halt.

—WILLIAM P. WADSWORTH, M.F.H., *RIDING TO HOUNDS IN AMERICA: AN INTRODUCTION FOR FOXHUNTERS*

"Black" ditches are full of dark murky water, the color of Guiness stout but hardly so tasty. Waiting your turn, watching horses and rider in front scrambling up the bank, only to slide back into the ditch and emerge, covered with black murky water, you ask yourself, Why am I doing this?

—JOY SLATER, WITH STEVEN D. PRICE, *RIDING'S A JOY*

Then, for the first time, I heard a sound which has thrilled fox-hunters to their marrow. From the far side of the wood came the long shrill screech (for which it is impossible to find an adequate word) which signifies that one of the [whippers-in] has viewed the fox quitting the covert. "Gone away" it meant.

—SIEGFRIED SASSOON, *MEMOIRS OF A FOX-HUNTING MAN*

A fox-hunt to a foreigner is strange;
'T is also subject to the double danger
Of tumbling first, and having in exchange
Some pleasant jesting at the awkward stranger:
But Juan had been early taught to range
The wilds, as doth an Arab turn'd avenger,
So that his horse, or charger, hunter, hack,
Knew that he had a rider on his back.

And now in this new field, with some applause,
He clear'd hedge, ditch, and double post, and rail,
And never craned, and made but few "faux pas,"
And only fretted when the scent 'gan fail.
He broke, 't is true, some statutes of the laws
Of hunting—for the sagest youth is frail;
Rode o'er the hounds, it may be, now and then,
And once o'er several country gentlemen.

But on the whole, to general admiration
He acquitted both himself and horse: the squires
Marvell'd at merit of another nation;
The boors cried "Dang it? who'd have thought it?"—
    Sires,
The Nestors of the sporting generation,
Swore praises, and recall'd their former fires;
The huntsman's self relented to a grin,
And rated him almost a whipper-in.

        —GEORGE GORDON NOEL, LORD BYRON, *DON JUAN*

The English gentleman galloping after a fox—the un-speakable in full pursuit of the uneatable.

        —OSCAR WILDE, *A WOMAN OF NO IMPORTANCE*

But in whatever garb the hunting parson may ride, he almost invariably rides well, and always enjoys the sport. If he did not, what would tempt him to run counter, as he does, to his bishop and the old ladies? And though, when the hounds are first dashing out of covert, and when the sputtering is beginning and the eager impetuosity of the young is driving men three at a time into the same gap, when that wild excitement of a fox just away is at its height, and ordinary sportsmen are rushing for places, though at these moments the hunting parson may be able to restrain himself, and to declare by his momentary tranquillity that he is only there to see the hounds, he will ever be found, seeing the hounds also, when many of that eager crowd have lagged behind, altogether out of sight of the last tail of them.

—ANTHONY TROLLOPE, *HUNTING SKETCHES*

And I've followed John Peel both often and far
O'er the rasper fence and the gate and the bar,
From Low Denton Holme up to Scratchmere Scar,
As we vied for the brush in the morning.

(Chorus) 'Twas the sound of his horn called me from
      my bed,
And the cry of his hounds has me oft-times led,
For Peel's View-halloo would waken the dead,
Or a fox from his lair in the morning.

—JOHN WOODCOCK GRAVES, "JOHN PEEL"

Now leave the chair upon the grass:
Bring hound and huntsman here,
And I on this strange road will pass,
Fill full of ancient cheer.

—WILLIAM BUTLER YEATS, "THE BALLAD OF THE FOXHUNTER"

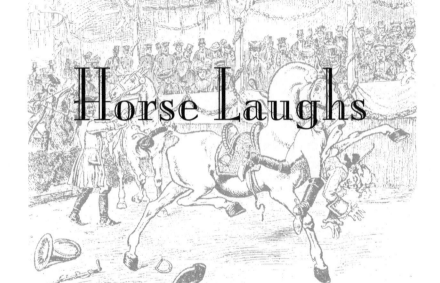

Horse Laughs

I never play horseshoes 'cause Mother taught us not to throw our clothes around.

—MR. ED [THE "TALKING HORSE" OF THE 1960s TV SERIES]

Ignorance, Madam, pure ignorance.

SAMUEL JOHNSON, ON BEING ASKED HOW HE CAME TO DEFINE *PASTERN* IN HIS DICTIONARY AS "THE KNEE OF A HORSE"

Paying alimony is like feeding hay to a dead horse.

—ATTRIBUTED TO GROUCHO MARX

If the world was truly a rational place, men would ride sidesaddle.

—RITA MAE BROWN

I once bet on a horse that was so slow, I bet it to live.

I played a great horse yesterday! It took seven horses to beat him.

The horse I bet on was so slow, the jockey kept a diary of the trip.

My horse's jockey was hitting the horse. The horse turns around and says "Why are you hitting me, there is nobody behind us!"

That was the first time I saw a horse start from a kneeling position!

My horse was so late getting home, he tiptoed into the stable.

I don't mind when my horse is left at the post. I don't mind when my horse comes up to me in the stands and asks "Which way do I go?" But when the horse I bet on is at the $2 window betting on another horse in the same race . . .

—HENNY YOUNGMAN

Horse crazy. It happens to a lot of little girls. I think my case was fairly modest considering the more virulent strains of this epizootic. When I watched cowboy movies (and God knows I'm still a sucker for a Republic Western), it was the horse that held me in thrall. And while I had guns and holsters aplenty, my interest wasn't in the gunfight at the OK Corral, but riding off into the sunset on Topper, or Champion, or Trigger. Tarzan, Diablo, or Silver.

— CANDYCE BARNES, "BOOTS, SADDLE, TO HOME, AND AWAY," IN *HORSE PEOPLE*, EDITED BY MICHAEL J. ROSEN

[Topper, Champion, Trigger, Tarzan, Diablo, and Silver were the horses of cowboy movie heroes Hopalong Cassidy, Gene Autry, Roy Rogers, Ken Maynard, the Cisco Kid, and the Lone Ranger, respectively.]

The Braiding Bunch.

—T-SHIRT WORN BY A HORSE-SHOW GROOM

And if you please, one that can show . . . just locally of
course,
Perhaps a little Medal/Maclay or equitation horse.
Of course, I really wouldn't mind if I found out that you
had sent
A horse to hunt and show and hack and perhaps three-
day event.

—COOKY MCCLUNG, "DEAR SANTA," IN HORSEFOLK ARE
DIFFERENT

My experience of horses is that they never throw away a
chance to go lame, and that in all respects they are well
meaning and unreliable animals. I have also observed
that if you refuse a high price for a favorite horse, he will
go and lay down somewhere and die.

—MARK TWAIN, IN THE SAN FRANCISCO BULLETIN

I know the horse too well. I have known the horse in war and in peace, and there is no place where a horse is comfortable. A horse thinks of too many things to do which you do not expect. He is apt to bite you in the leg when you think he is half asleep. The horse has too many caprices, and he is too much given to initiative. He invents too many new ideas. No, I don't want anything to do with a horse.

—MARK TWAIN, *SPEECHES*

. . . I am not an expert in horses and do not speak with assurance. I can always tell which is the front end of a horse, but beyond that, my art is not above the ordinary.

—MARK TWAIN, *A BIOGRAPHY*

If the horses knew their strength we should not ride anymore.

—MARK TWAIN, *NOTEBOOK #42*

I am one of the poorest horsemen in the world, and I never mount a horse without experiencing a sort of dread that I may be setting out on that last mysterious journey which all of us must take sooner or later, and I never come back in safety from a horseback trip without thinking of my latter end for two or three days afterward.

—QUOTED IN *MARK TWAIN IN HAWAII* BY WALTER FRANCIS FREAR

I realize that the concept of wild horses probably stirs romantic notions in many of you, but this is because you have never met any wild horses in person. In person, they are like enormous hooved rats. They amble up to your camp site, and their attitude is: "We're wild horses. We're going to eat your food, knock down your tent and poop on your shoes. We're protected by federal law, just like Richard Nixon."

—DAVE BARRY, "TENTING GRANDPA BOB"

There you are, $600,000 on four hooves. I bet a Russian Czar never paid that kind of dough for a single horse.

—THE GODFATHER [FILM VERSION, 1972, SCREENPLAY BY FRANCIS FORD COPPOLA]

My dear, I don't care what they do, so long as they don't do it in the street and frighten the horses.

—MRS. PATRICK CAMPBELL, ENGLISH ACTRESS OF THE EARLY TWENTIETH CENTURY

———

Certain comic effects can be achieved by a brand-new rider, especially a man who dresses like a fashion model and rides like a tailor.

—C. J. J. MULLEN

———

I've spent most of my life riding horses. The rest I've just wasted.

—ANONYMOUS

In what other sport do you put on leather boots, stretch-fabric breeches, a shirt and tie, a wool jacket, a velvet-covered cap, and leather gloves, and *then* go out and exercise?

—A. LONDON WOLF [ON HORSE SHOWING IN NINETY-PLUS-DEGREE SUMMER WEATHER]

I ride horses because it's the only sport where I can exercise while sitting down.

—JOAN HANSEN

Horses do think. Not very deeply, perhaps, but enough to get you into a lot of trouble.

—PATRICIA JACOBSON AND MARCIA HAYES, *A HORSE AROUND THE HOUSE*

Anyone who is concerned about his dignity would be well advised to keep away from horses.

—Prince Philip, Duke of Edinburgh

People on horses look better than they are. People in cars look worse than they are.

—Marya Mannes

I'd horsewhip you . . . if I had a horse.

—Groucho Marx (as Professor Quincey Adams Wagstaff) in the movie *Horse Feathers*

I have the experience to be Governor. I know how to play craps. I know how to play poker. I know how to go in and out of the Baptist Church and ride horses.

—Governor Earl Long

Look, Mommy, he's wearing bell-bottoms!

—SMALL CHILD'S REACTION TO SEEING A CLYDESDALE'S FETLOCK "FEATHERS"

The old mare watched the tractor work
A thing of rubber and steel,
Ready to follow the slightest wish
Of the man who held the wheel.
She said to herself as it passed by,
You gave me an awful jolt
But there's still one thing you cannot do,
You cannot raise a colt.

—ANONYMOUS

Riding: The art of keeping a horse between you and the ground.

—ANONYMOUS

You can tell a gelding, you can ask a mare, but you must discuss it with a stallion.

—ANONYMOUS

Speak kindly to your little horse,
And soothe him when he wheezes,
Or he may turn his back on you,
And kick you where he pleases.

—ANONYMOUS

The daughter who won't lift a finger in the house is the same child who cycles madly off in the pouring rain to spend all morning mucking out a stable.

—SARAH ARMSTRONG

I know two things about the horse,
And one of them is rather coarse.

—ANONYMOUS

A horse is dangerous at both ends and uncomfortable in the middle.

—IAN FLEMING, QUOTED IN THE SUNDAY *TIMES* (LONDON),
OCTOBER 9, 1966

One man's wrong lead is another man's counter-canter.

—STEVEN D. PRICE

Want to end up with a million bucks in the horse business? Start out with five million.

—ANONYMOUS

A camel is a horse designed by a committee.

—ATTRIBUTED TO BRITISH ECONOMIST ALEC ISSIGORIS

To confess that you are totally ignorant about the horse is social suicide: you will be despised by everybody, especially the horse.

—W. C. SELLAR, *HORSE NONSENSE*

How do you catch a loose horse? Make a noise like a carrot.

—BRITISH CAVALRY JOKE

An exhibitor went up to a horse show judge to complain about being placed below someone who made some sort of mistake, such as being on the wrong lead.

The judge's explanation: "the other guy did it better wrong than you did it right."
—ANONYMOUS

I prefer a bike to a horse. The brakes are more easily checked.

—LAMBERT JEFFRIES

His registered name is Lord Bob, but I call him Bob, Mr. Roberto, or Mush. Sometimes it seems as though I hocked my life to buy him.

—SHAN N. CUTCLIFF, QUOTED IN *HORSES AND THEIR WOMEN* BY BARBARA COHN AND LOUISE TAYLOR

Well, the hillbillies beat the dudes and took the polo championship of the world right out of the drawing room and into the bunkhouse. And she won't go East in years.

Poor old society. They got nothing exclusive left. The movie folks outmarried and outdivorced 'em, the common folks took their cocktails, 'near' society took to bridge. Now polo has gone to the buckwheat belt.

—WILL ROGERS, IN A 1933 SYNDICATED NEWSPAPER COLUMN, AFTER A TEAM OF WESTERN POLO PLAYERS SOUNDLY DEFEATED A TEAM OF THE BEST OF THE EASTERN "ESTABLISHMENT" PLAYERS

Somewhere there must be a distance!

—CAPTION OF AN R. W. MUTCH CARTOON

She couldn't ride a freight train out of Kansas!

—REMARK BY A DISGUSTED TRAINER WATCHING HIS STUDENT

You can lead a horse to water, but if you can teach him to roll over and float on his back, then you got something.

—Joe E. Lewis

That hoss wasn't built to tread the earth,
He took natural to the air,
And every time he went aloft,
He tried to leave me there.

—Anonymous Tribute to an Unmanageable Horse

8

Horse Truths

And God took a handful of southerly wind, blew his breath over it and created the horse.

—BEDOUIN LEGEND

———•••••———

A horse cannot gain weight if not fed with extra fodder during the night; a man cannot become wealthy without earnings apart from his regular salaries.

—CHINESE PROVERB

———•••••———

Time is the rider that breaks youth.

—GEORGE HERBERT, *JACULA PRUDENTUM*

———•••••———

He that will venture nothing must not get on horse-back.

—C. J. APPERLEY [NIMROD], *QUARTERLY REVIEW*

A prince is never surrounded by as much majesty on his throne as he is on a beautiful horse.

—WILLIAM CAVENDISH, DUKE OF NEWCASTLE, *A GENERAL SYSTEM OF HORSEMANSHIP IN ALL ITS BRANCHES*

The true character of the horse is never completely revealed in the stable or in the riding school, beneath the saddle or in harness. To know him as he really is we must watch him under the open sky, in the meadow, among his own kind, for there we can see how different each horse is from his companions, how the ancient law of the herd lives on, and how the hierarchy is created with barely an encounter.

—HANS-HEINRICH ISENBART, *THE BEAUTY OF THE HORSE*

An owner [of a Tennessee Walking Horse] once said that his horse reminded him of a lightning rod, for, as he rode, all the sorrows of his heart flowed down through the splendid muscles of his horse and were grounded in the earth.

—MARGUERITE HENRY, *ALBUM OF HORSES*

For many of us, the horse is a symbol of what is right with the world. In spite of generations of careful breeding, the horse still seems to be a step or two out of the wild. In spite of training and confinement, the horse at gallop seems to be a step or two from freedom.

—SHARON B. SMITH, *THE AFFORDABLE HORSE*

Never fight the oats.

—WILLIAM STEINKRAUS, *REFLECTIONS ON RIDING AND JUMPING*

Those who look down eventually get there.

—Kip Rosenthal

I sit astride life like a bad rider on a horse. I only owe it to the horse's good nature that I am not thrown off at this very moment.

—Austrian philosopher Ludwig Wittgenstien

God forbid that I should go to any heaven in which there are no horses.

—R. B. Cunninghame-Graham, in a letter to President Theodore Roosevelt

---

It is not enough for a man to know how to ride; he must know how to fall.

—Mexican proverb

There is something about the outside of a horse that is good for the inside of a man.

—Sir Winston Churchill [also attributed to another British Prime Minister, Lord Palmerston]

[When this quote once appeared in *The Chronicle of the Horse* magazine, it had the following typo: There is something about the outside of a horse that is good for the inside of a mare.]

A canter is the cure for every evil.

—Benjamin Disraeli, *The Young Duke*

Many people have sighed for the 'good old days' and regretted the 'passing of the horse,' but today, when only those who like horses own them, it is a far better time for horses.

—C. W. Anderson, *The Complete Book of Horses and Horsemanship*

A man may well bring a horse to the water, But he cannot make him drink without he will.

A short horse is soon curried.

—JOHN HEYWOOD, "PROVERBS"

———•·•·•———

A man on a horse is spiritually as well as physically bigger than a man on foot.

—JOHN STEINBECK, "THE RED PONY"

———•·•·•———

The wagon rests in winter, the sleigh in summer, the horse never.

—YIDDISH PROVERB

No ride is ever the last one. No horse is ever the last one you will have. Somehow there will always be other horses, other places to ride them.

—MONICA DICKENS, *TALKING OF HORSES*

In buying a horse or taking a wife, shut your eyes tight and commend yourself to God.

—TUSCAN PROVERB

The horse is God's gift to man.

—ARABIAN PROVERB

Show me your horse and I will tell you who you are.

—ENGLISH PROVERB

Dog lovers hate to clean out kennels. Horse lovers like cleaning stables.

—MONICA DICKENS, *TALKING OF HORSES*

To ride a horse well, you have to know it as well as you know your best friend.

—GRAND PRIX SHOW-JUMPING RIDER KATIE MONAHAN PRUDENT, IN A ROLEX ADVERTISEMENT

There is no secret so close as that between a rider and his horse.

—ROBERT SMITH SURTEES, *MR. SPONGE'S SPORTING TOUR*

Nothing on four legs is quicker than a horse heading back to the barn.

—PAMELA C. BIDDLE AND JOEL E. FISHMAN, *ALL I NEED TO KNOW I LEARNED FROM MY HORSE*

The ears never lie.

—Don Burt

The sun it was, ye glittering gods, ye took to make a horse.

—Dirga-Tamas

You will find it is always easier to walk if there is a horse between your legs.

—Anonymous

When the horse's jaws are in motion, his mind is at rest.

—Pete Rose

Old minds are like old horses; you must exercise them if you wish to keep them in working order.

—JOHN ADAMS, SECOND PRESIDENT OF THE UNITED STATES

The stable wears out a horse more than the road does.

—FRENCH PROVERB

Horses leave hoofprints on your heart.

—ANONYMOUS

Some people have animal eyes—bears' eyes, cats' eyes, pigs' eyes, but horses have human eyes and I love horses better than people.

—JOSÉ GARCIA VILLA

A horse is a thing of such beauty . . . none will tire of looking at him as long as he displays himself in his splendor.

—XENOPHON, *ON HORSEMANSHIP*

God first made Man. He thought better of it and made Woman. When He got time He made the Horse, which has the courage and spirit of Man and the beauty and grace of Woman.

—BRAZILIAN SAYING

The air of heaven is that which blows between a horse's ears.

—ARABIAN PROVERB

. . . This most noble beast is the most beautiful, the swiftest and of the highest courage of domesticated animals. His long mane and tail adorn and beautify him. He is of a fiery temperament, but good tempered, obedient, docile and well-mannered.

—PEDRO GARCIA CONDE, 1685

We have almost forgotten how strange a thing it is that so huge and powerful and intelligent an animal as a horse should allow another, and far more feeble animal, to ride upon its back.

—PETER GRAY

Gypsy gold does not chink and glitter. It gleams in the sun and neighs in the dark.

—GYPSY SAYING

There is something about riding down the street on a prancing horse that makes you feel like something, even when you ain't a thing.

—WILL ROGERS

Every horse thinks his own pack the heaviest.

—ANONYMOUS

Speak your mind, but ride a fast horse.

—ANONYMOUS

Because we have the best hay and the best oats and the best horses.

—COL. SIR HARRY LLEWELLYN, *PASSPORTS TO LIFE* [RECALLING HIS ANSWER WHEN ASKED WHY THE BRITISH SHOW-JUMPING TEAM WAS SO SUCCESSFUL IN THE 1952 OLYMPICS]

A good rider on a good horse is as much above himself and others as the world can make him.

—EDWARD, LORD HERBERT, *AUTOBIOGRAPHY*

I really like his character. If he was a person now, he'd be my best friend.

—GRAND PRIX RIDER IAN MILLAR, TALKING ABOUT HIS HORSE BIG BEN

Horses change lives. They give our young people confidence and self esteem. They provide peace and tranquility to troubled souls—they give us hope!

—TONI ROBINSON

A Hibernian sage once wrote that there are three things a man never forgets: The girl of his early youth, a devoted teacher, and a great horse.

—C. J. J. MULLEN

A fine little smooth horse colt,
Should move a man as much as doth a son.

—THOMAS KYD

The horse through all its trials has preserved the sweetness of paradise in its blood.

—JOHANNES JENSEN

We gaze upon their quiet beauty, their natural elegance, and we are captivated. They see us softly, in gentle light ... rewarding human companionship with strength, grace and intelligence. As they run through arenas and open fields, past mountains and seas, moving like the wind toward heaven, we travel with them, if only in our hearts.

—Anonymous

Wherever man has left his footprint in the long ascent from barbarism to civilization, we will find the hoofprint of a horse beside it.

—John Trotwood Moore

I saw a child who couldn't walk, sit on a horse and laugh and talk . . . I saw a child who could only crawl, mount a horse and sit up tall . . . I saw a child born into strife, take up and hold the reins of life . . . And that same child was heard to say, thank you God for showing me the way.

—JOHN ANTHONY DAVIS

Look back on our struggle for freedom,
Trace our present day strength to its source,
And you'll find that man's pathway to glory,
Is strewn with the bones of a horse.

—ANONYMOUS

He that hath love in his heart hath spurs in his sides.

—ENGLISH PROVERB

Horses and poets should be fed, not overfed.

—CHARLES II OF ENGLAND

Never give up. For fifty years they said the horse was through. Now look at him—a status symbol.

—FLETCHER KNEBEL

The wind flew. God told the wind to condense itself and out of the flurry came the horse. But with the spark of spirit the horse flew by the wind itself.

—MARGUERITE HENRY, *KING OF THE WIND*

A horse already knows how to be a horse; the rider has to learn how to become a rider. A horse without a rider is still a horse; a rider without a horse is no longer a rider.

—ANONYMOUS

We all want everything to be wonderful. Every woman wants to sit upon a horse dressed in bells and go riding off through the boundless green and sensual forest.

—CLARISSA ESTES, *WOMEN WHO RUN WITH THE WOLVES*

In grateful and reverent memory of the Empire's horses (some 375,000) who fell in the Great War (1914–1918). Most obediently, and often most painfully, they died.

—MEMORIAL AT CHURCH OF ST. JUDE, LONDON

To be loved by a horse, or by any animal, should fill us with awe—for we have not deserved it.

—Marion Garretty

A horse loves freedom, and the weariest old work horse will roll on the ground or break into a lumbering gallop when he is turned loose into the open.

—Gerald Raferty

Sell the cow, buy the sheep, but never be without the horse.

—Irish proverb

My horse has a hoof of striped agate. His fetlock is like fine eagle plume. His legs are like quick lightning. My horse has a tail like a trailing black cloud. His mane is made of short rainbows. My horse's eyes are made of big stars.

—Navajo war god's horse song

The horse is a creature who sacrifices his own being to exist through the will of another . . . he is the noble conquest of man.

—Georges Louis Leclerc, Comte de Buffon

No one can teach riding so well as a horse.

—C. S. LEWIS

Spring and summer are riding on a piebald mare.

—RUSSIAN PROVERB

My horses are my friends, not my slaves.

—DR. REINER KLIMKE

There are times when you can trust a horse, times when you can't, and times when you have to.

—ANONYMOUS

Here lies the body of my good horse, The General. For years he bore me around the circuit of my practice and all that time he never made a blunder. Would that his master could say the same.

—President John Tyler's epitaph for his horse

An old friend is like a saddled horse.

—Afghanistani proverb

Once a horse is born, someone will be found to ride it.

—Hebrew proverb

Raise your horse as a son, ride him as an enemy.

—Arabian proverb

One can't shoe a running horse.

—DUTCH PROVERB

As old wood is best to burn; old horses to ride; old books to read; old wine to drink; so are old friends most trusty to use.

—LEONARD WRIGHT

The horses of hope gallop, but the asses of experience go slowly.

—RUSSIAN PROVERB

One must plow with the horses one has.

—GERMAN PROVERB

What the colt learns in youth he continues in old age.

—FRENCH PROVERB

Care, and not fine stables, makes a good horse.

—DANISH PROVERB

Who buys a horse buys care.

—SPANISH PROVERB

A little neglect may breed mischief: for want of a nail the shoe was lost; for want of a shoe the horse was lost; and for want of a horse the rider was lost.

—BENJAMIN FRANKLIN, *POOR RICHARD'S ALMANACK* [ALSO FOUND IN *JACULA PRUDENTUM* BY GEORGE HERBERT]

If you ride a horse, sit close and tight,
If you ride a man, sit easy and light.

He that riseth late, must trot all day, and shall scarce
overtake his business at night.

—BENJAMIN FRANKLIN, *POOR RICHARD'S ALMANACK*

The child who is fortunate enough to be associated
with horses during his formative years can look back
on fond memories, and those who continue to ride,
hunt, or show during their lifetime seldom experience
anything more gratifying than the thrill of winning
their first ribbon.

—STEPHEN O. HAWKINS, IN *LEARNING TO RIDE, HUNT, AND SHOW*
BY GORDON WRIGHT

The horse is both intelligent enough and stupid enough to do what we demand of him.

—GEORGE GAYLORD SIMPSON, *HORSES*

While there are many things you can fake through in this life, pretending that you know horses when you don't isn't one of them.

—COOKY MCCLUNG, *HORSEFOLK ARE DIFFERENT*

The horse loves his oats more than his saddle.

—RUSSIAN PROVERB

Of all creatures, the horse is the noblest.

—GERVASE MARKHAM, *THE COMPLEAT HORSEMAN*

For the student there is, in its season, no better place than the saddle.

—FRANCIS PARKMAN, *AUTOBIOGRAPHY*

Fat is the best color.

—HORSEMAN'S ADAGE

You sometimes hear the old saying "Fat is the best color." This means, of course, that fat covers a multitude of conformation faults and therefore *looks* good—especially to the less discerning horseman.

—ELEANOR F. PRINCE AND GAYDELL M. COLLIER, *BASIC HORSE CARE*

Watching a seasoned pony carry its young rider, one senses the pony is doing the teaching. With an uncanny sense of the rider's limitations and often genuine kindness, ponies seem to possess an intelligence you don't always see in horses.

—NINA DURAN, *A PONY RIDER'S DIARY*

Let us put Germany in the saddle, so to speak—it already knows how to ride.

—OTTO VON BISMARCK, IN A SPEECH TO THE GERMAN REICHSTAG

Some of my best leading men have been dogs and horses.

—ELIZABETH TAYLOR

Words are as beautiful as wild horses, and sometimes as difficult to corral.

—TED BERKMAN, IN THE *CHRISTIAN SCIENCE MONITOR*

Human reason is like a drunken man on horseback; set it up on one side and it tumbles over on the other.

—MARTIN LUTHER

Not the fastest horse can catch a word spoken in anger.

—CHINESE PROVERB

A good resolution is like an old horse: often saddled but rarely ridden.

—MEXICAN PROVERB

If there's a horse, you can always find a whip.

—YIDDISH PROVERB

Competitions are for horses, not for artists.

—ATTRIBUTED TO COMPOSER BELA BARTOK

Of all Creatures God made at the Creation, there is none except man more excellent, or so much to be respected as a Horse.

—BEDOUIN LEGEND

A horse shoe that clatters needs a nail.

—SPANISH PROVERB

A good horse makes short miles.

—ENGLISH PROVERB

—•••—

Ride a cow until you ride a horse.

—JAPANESE PROVERB [MEANING: MAKE DO WITH WHAT YOU CAN GET UNTIL SOMETHING BETTER COMES ALONG]

—•••—

Ride on horseback, go around with the person.

— JAPANESE PROVERB [MEANING: ONE SHOULD SPEAK ONLY FROM ONE'S OWN EXPERIENCES]

—•••—

Hurry! At a gallop! To Paradise!

—THE LAST WORDS OF MADAME LOUISE, DAUGHTER OF LOUIS XV OF FRANCE

To finish is to win.

—ENDURANCE-RIDING MOTTO

I speak Spanish to God, Italian to women, French to men and German to my horse.

—CHARLES V, HOLY ROMAN EMPEROR

A nod is as good as a wink to a blind horse.

—IRISH PROVERB

One must get off one's horse over its head; to step off is merely weak.

—MAO TSE-TUNG

[The horse possesses] a singular body and a noble spirit, the principle thereof is a loving and dutiful inclination to the service of Man, wherein he never faileth in Peace nor War . . . and therefore . . . we must needs account it the most noble and necessary of all four-footed Beasts.

—EDWARD TOPSEL, QUOTED IN *HORSEWATCHING* BY DESMOND MORRIS

To be an equestrian in the classical sense is not to be just a rider. It is a position in life. It is a stance we take in relation to life. We must make a choice between self-love, the promotion of our own well-being of our ego, and love for the horse. That is the fundamental attitudinal decision that earned Xenophon the title Father of Classical Dressage: he dared to love a horse!

—CHARLES DE KUNFFY, *TRAINING STRATEGIES FOR DRESSAGE RIDERS*

Never threaten to take away a kid's horse, unless you don't care if they start trusting horses more than you. If a young person is having or causing trouble, the horse may be their salvation.

—LESLI K. GROVES, "KIDS & HORSES: RATED PG-17," IN *AMERICA'S HORSE* MAGAZINE

———•••••———

Don't ride the high horse. The fall, when it comes, is hard.

—AMERICAN PROVERB

The American Saddle Horse, with his refinement of gaits and his animation and beauty, does not belong just to his owner or trainer. He belongs to the show ring, where he can bring joy and thrill to thousands of "ringside riders."

—MARGUERITE HENRY, *ALBUM OF HORSES*

The speed of a runaway horse counts for nothing.

—ARTIST JEAN COCTEAU

Soft grass for an old horse.

—Bulgarian proverb

———•••———

Polo is a disease for which poverty is the only cure.

—Anonymous

———•••———

The substitution of the internal combustion engine for the horse marked a very gloomy milestone in the progress of mankind.

—Sir Winston Churchill

For centuries we have been famed for our skill in horsemanship, so that the Magyar has no need to have his horses dance with crossed legs, Spanish fashion.

—KING MATHIAS I CORVINUS OF HUNGARY, TO HIS FATHER-IN-LAW, THE KING OF NAPLES, WHO HAD SENT HIM A SPANISH RIDING MASTER

The Budweiser Clydesdales! I'm so glad to see you. Now that John Wayne and Elvis are gone, you're all we have left!

—CB MESSAGE FROM A DRIVER WHO SAW THE VANS PULLING THE BUDWEISER CLYDESDALES, QUOTED IN *ALL THE KING'S HORSES* BY ALIX COLEMAN AND STEVEN D. PRICE

My horse be swift in flight even like a bird,
My horse be swift in flight.
Bear me now in safety far from the enemy's arrows.
And you shall be rewarded with streamers and ribbons
    red.

—SIOUX WARRIOR'S SONG TO HIS HORSE

———

Love means attention, which means looking after the
things we love. We call it stable management.

—GEORGE H. MORRIS, *THE AMERICAN JUMPING STYLE*

The horse that pulls the most is usually given the least amount of oats.

—GERMAN PROVERB

———•+•+•———

I haven't been able to ride very much since my hip operation several years ago. I think I would still be playing polo if I hadn't had that. If I ever got to where I couldn't ride, I don't think I'd live very long.

—CECIL SMITH [GENERALLY CONSIDERED TO HAVE BEEN AMERICA'S MOST OUTSTANDING POLO PLAYER; HE PLAYED HIS LAST POLO GAME AT AGE EIGHTY-THREE AND LAST RODE AT NINETY-THREE]

———•+•+•———

The limping horse falls behind.

—DUTCH PROVERB

There on the tips of fair fresh flowers feedeth he;
how joyous is his neigh,
There, in the midst of sacred pollen hidden, all is he;
how joyous is his neigh.

—NAVAJO SONG

One reason why birds and horses are not unhappy is because they are not trying to impress other birds and horses.

—DALE CARNEGIE, *HOW TO WIN FRIENDS AND INFLUENCE PEOPLE*

With horses and warriors, you can't judge from their appearance.

—JAPANESE PROVERB

Put the horse before the cart.

—ENGLISH PROVERB

No horseman or horsewoman has ever finished learning.

—MARY GORDON-WATSON, *THE HANDBOOK OF RIDING*

A wise horse cares not how fast a man may run.

—ARMENIAN PROVERB

If the horse is good, you don't mind paying the rental fee.

—JAPANESE PROVERB

When two ride a horse, one must ride behind.

—ENGLISH PROVERB

The empire was won on horseback, but you cannot govern on horseback.

—CHINESE GENERAL YEH-LU T'SU T'SAI, QUOTED IN *THE HORSE THROUGH FIFTY CENTURIES OF CIVILIZATION* BY ANTHONY DENT

Old horses for young riders, old riders for young horses.

—HORSEMAN'S PROVERB

Nature will never disclose all her secrets to us, and the horse will forever have in store for us novelties, surprises, springing from life itself.

—GEN. ALEXIS L'HOTTE, *QUESTIONS EQUESTRES*, QUOTED IN
EQUITATION: LEARNING AND TEACHING BY JEAN FROISSARD

Horses are karmic and they come to us in our lives karmically, when it is time for us truly to learn.

—DOMINIQUE BARBIER, WITH MARY DANIELS,
DRESSAGE FOR THE NEW AGE

In order to go fast, one must go slow.

—OLD HORSEMAN'S PROVERB

Do not mistake a goat's beard for a fine stallion's tail.

—IRISH PROVERB

There is a natural affinity between women and horses, something so basic it creates an immediate foundation for a relationship and a launching pad for almost everything we want to do with a horse.

—MARY D. MIDKIFF, *FITNESS, PERFORMANCE AND THE FEMALE EQUESTRIAN*

One white foot—buy him,
Two white feet—try him;
Three white feet—look well about him,
Four white feet—go without him.

—OLD HORSE-BUYING PREJUDICE

Tell it to the Horse Marines.

—OLD SAYING

Never change horses in midstream.

War is no place for horses.

—BRITISH SHOW-JUMPING RIDER AND HORSE-SHOW ORGANIZER
COL. SIR MIKE ANSELL, *SOLDIER ON*

Never change horses in midstream.

—OLD ADAGE [SIMILARLY: NEVER SWAP HORSES CROSSING A
STREAM]

A mule is an animal that has neither pride of ancestry nor hope of posterity.

—ANONYMOUS

———•••••———

For bringing us the horse we could almost forgive you for bringing us whiskey. Horses make a landscape more beautiful.

—LAME DEER, QUOTED IN *HORSES MAKE A LANDSCAPE MORE BEAUTIFUL* BY ALICE WALKER

———•••••———

Heretofore, every peasant knew only too well that when he had a horse he could manage his homestead and that without a horse he could not make a living . . .

—NIKITA KHRUSHCHEV, IN A SPEECH TO THE COMMUNIST PARTY CONGRESS

When the horse dies, dismount.

—Anonymous

Talking to a horse's ear.

—Japanese expression [meaning: to say something that falls on deaf ears]

But a horse is a labor of love as well as a responsibility, an aesthetic as well as a dynamic pleasure, something to contemplate as well as to ride.

—Sarah Montague, in *A Rider's Diary* by Nina Duran`

Horses are something to dream about . . . and to wish for; fun to watch . . . and to make friends with; nice to pat . . . and great to hug: and, oh, what a joy to ride!

—DOROTHY HENDERSON PINCH, *HAPPY HORSEMANSHIP*

The slow horse reaches the mill.

—IRISH PROVERB

It's difficult to water a horse that won't lower its head.

—FINNISH PROVERB

Straight from the horse's mouth.

—OLD EXPRESSION

Put a beggar on horseback and he'll ride to hell.

[And:]

Put a beggar on horseback and he'll go on a gallop.

—IRISH PROVERBS

When I hear somebody talk about a horse or a cow being stupid, I figure it's a sure sign that animal has outfoxed them.

—TOM DORANCE

Stable thinking is the ability to say "neigh."
—SOURCE UNKNOWN

An old horse finds its way best.
—NORWEGIAN PROVERB

A loose horse will always be found at the barn.
—INDIAN PROVERB

You can lead a horse to water . . . if you got a horse.
—ENGLISH PROVERB

The first horse to drink doesn't get dirty water.

—NIGERIAN PROVERB

Dead horses don't kick.

—BULGARIAN PROVERB

The horse's death makes the cow fatter.

— ENGLISH PROVERB

Go, sir, and gallop, and don't forget the world was made in six days. You can ask me for anything except time.

—NAPOLEON BONAPARTE, TO AN AIDE

A bad foaling might still produce a fine horse.

—FRENCH PROVERB

Folk songs? They're all *folk* songs—I never heard a horse sing.

—LOUIS "SATCHMO" ARMSTRONG [ALSO ATTRIBUTED TO FOLKSINGER WOODY GUTHRIE]

When the mule is beaten, the horse is scared.

—CHINESE PROVERB

There is no greater pleasure than a nice ride on a nice horse on a beautiful day.

—JUDY RICHTER, *PONY TALK*

May your descendants ride in chariots.

—CHINESE GOOD LUCK WISH

The horse is, like man, the most beautiful and the most miserable of creatures.

—ROSA BONHEUR

Horses have hoofs to carry them over frost and snow; hair, to protect them from wind and cold. They eat grass and drink water, and fling up their heels over the campaign. Such is the real nature of horses. Palatial dwellings are of no use to them.

—CHUANG TZU

Men are not hanged for stealing horses, but that horses may not be stolen.

—GEORGE SAVILE, MARQUESS OF HALIFAX, *REFLECTIONS*

A donkey appears to me like a horse translated into Dutch.

—GEORG CHRISTOPH LICHTENBERG

It is not the duty of the horse to be a biofeedback mechanism for yearning humans; yet it is remarkable how consistently people with horses claimed to have learned much about themselves through them. Certainly, the management of a horse will give you a rapid evaluation of your patience, your powers of concentration, and your ability to hold on to delicate ideas for sustained periods of time.

—THOMAS MCGUANE, *SOME HORSES*

From a workaday drudge, [the Shetland pony] became a fun-loving playmate. No door was closed to him, for he had taught himself how to slide bolts, open gates, rattle latches. His long lips became expert at plucking caps from children's heads or handkerchiefs from pockets.

—MARGUERITE HENRY, *ALBUM OF HORSES*

Being born in a stable does not make a man a horse.

> —ARTHUR WELLSELEY, DUKE OF WELLINGTON [ON LEARNING HE HAD BEEN DESCRIBED AS IRISH BECAUSE HE HAD BEEN BORN IN DUBLIN]

Lend a horse, and you may have back his skin.

> —ENGLISH PROVERB

The primeval instincts of the horse are nowhere more pronounced than in the bond between the mare and her foal, for the maternal instinct is the strongest in nature. It is this instinct that ensures the survival of the species and determines the character of the mare and her attitude toward other horses and toward man.

—HANS-HEINRICH ISENBART, *THE BEAUTY OF THE HORSE*

Men are better when riding, more just and more understanding, and more alert and more at ease and more under-taking, and better knowing of all countries and all passages . . .

—EDWARD, DUKE OF YORK

Reason lies between the spur and the bridle.

    —GEORGE HERBERT, *JACULA PRUDENTUM*

Never gallop Pegasus to death.

    —ALEXANDER POPE, "EPISTLE I, PROLOGUE TO THE IMITATIONS OF HORACE"

I have thought that to breed a noble horse is to share with God in one of His mysteries, as well as one of His delights.

    —TOM LEA, *THE HANDS OF CANTU*

A horse is worth more than riches.

—SPANISH PROVERB

Selected
Biographical
Notes

Ackerman, Diane. American poet and essayist.

Adams, John (1735–1826). Second president of the United States.

Addison, Joseph (1672–1719) and Richard Steele (1672–1729). English essayists, best known for *The Tatler* and *The Spectator*.

Aesop (620?–550? B.C.). Greek fabulist.

Agate, James (1877–1947). English writer.

Anderson, C. W. American equestrian author and illustrator.

Anderson, Sherwood (1876–1941). American author best known for *Winesberg, Ohio.*

Ansell, Col. Sir Mike (b. 1905). English military officer, horseman, and horse-show organizer.

Apperley, C. J. Eighteenth-century equestrian writer under the pen name Nimrod.

Armour, Richard. American writer and humorist.

Armstrong, Louis "Satchmo" (1900–1971). American jazz musician.

Arnold, Matthew (1822–1888). English poet and critic.

Asquith, Margot (1864–1945). British writer and personality.

Auel, Jean M. American author best known for *The Clan of the Cave Bear.*

Barbier, Dominique. Dressage rider, trainer, and author, born in France and now based in California.

Barich, Bill. American writer.

Barnes, Candyce. American novelist and short-story writer.

Barnes, Simon. Racing and equestrian columnist for the *Times* (London).

Barry, Dave. American humorist and columnist.

Bartok, Bela (1881–1945). Hungarian composer.

Bass, Rick. American writer of short stories, novels, and works of nonfiction.

Bates, Katharine Lee (1859–1929). American poet best known for "America the Beautiful."

Behan, Brendan (1923–1964). Irish dramatist.

Benét, Stephen Vincent (1898–1943). American poet and short-story writer, winner of a 1928 Pulitzer Prize.

Benét, William Rose (1886–1950). American poet.

Benson, Gary J. Contemporary American photographer.

Betjeman, Sir John (1906–1984). English poet; poet laureate 1972–1984.

Biddle, Pamela C., and Joel E. Fishman. Contemporary equestrian writers.

Bierce, Ambrose (1842–1914?). American writer.

Billings, Josh. Pen name of American humorist Henry Wheeler Shaw (1818–1885).

Bismarck, Otto von (1815–1898). German statesman.

Blackmore, R. D. (1825–1900). English novelist best known for *Lorna Doone*.

Blake, William (1757–1827). English poet and artist.

Blundeville, Thomas. Seventeeth-century horseman and writer.

Blunt, Wilfred Scawen (1840–1922). English poet, diplomat, and explorer.

Bonaparte, Napoleon (1769–1821). French military and political leader who as Napoleon I was emperor of France 1804–1815.

Bonheur, Rosa (1822–1898). French painter best known for *The Horse Fair.*

Boylen, Christilot Hanson. Dressage rider, trainer, and commentator.

Brainard, John. Nineteenth-century American poet.

Brannaman, Bob. American western trainer.

Brown, Rita Mae. American writer.

Browne, Sir Thomas (1605–1682). English author and physician.

Browning, Robert (1812–1889). English poet.

Buchwald, Art. American newspaper columnist and humorist, winner of a 1982 Pulitzer Prize.

Budiansky, Stephen. American anthropologist.

Buffon, Georges Louis Leclerc de (1707–1788). French naturalist.

Bulfinch's Mythology. The authoritative reference on classical myths and medieval fables by American writer and teacher Thomas Bulfinch (1796–1867).

Burn, Barbara. American editor and writer.

Burns, Robert (1759–1796). Scottish poet.

Burt, Don. American author, horse-show judge, and equestrian official; past president of the American Quarter Horse Association.

Butler, John. Nineteenth-century British horseman.

Byron, George Gordon Noel, Lord (1788–1824). English poet.

Camden, William (1551–1623). English poet.

Campbell, Mrs. Patrick (1865–1940). English actress.

Canty, Charlsie. American Thoroughbred racehorse trainer and TV commentator.

Carleton, William "Will" McKendree (1845–1912). American poet.

Carnegie, Dale (1888–1955). American businessman and author.

Carroll, Charles. Author of *Handicapping Speed.*

Carroll, Lewis. Pen name of Charles Lutwidge Dodgson (1832–1898), English writer best known for *Alice's Adventures in Wonderland* and *Through the Looking Glass.*

Cawain, Madison. Nineteenth-century American poet.

Chapman, Arthur (1873–1935). American poet.

Chapman, George (1559?–1634). English poet, dramatist, and translator.

Charles II (1630–1685). British king 1660–1685.

Charles V (1500–1558). Holy Roman Emperor.

Chaucer, Geoffrey (c. 1340–1400). English poet, best known for *The Canterbury Tales.*

Chuang Tzu (c. 300 B.C.). Chinese writer.

Churchill, Sir Winston (1874–1965). British statesman and author, winner of the 1953 Nobel Prize for literature.

Cocteau, Jean (1889–1963). French poet, playwright, and filmmaker.

Coleridge, Samuel Taylor (1772–1834). English poet.

Cowper, William (1731–1800). English poet.

Crabtree, Helen. A leading American saddle-seat horsemanship trainer and author.

cummings, e. e. (1894–1962). American poet.

Cunninghame-Graham, R. B. (1852–1936). Scottish-Spanish writer and historian.

Dante Alighieri (1265–1321). Italian poet, author of *The Divine Comedy.*

Davidson, John (1857–1909). Scottish poet.

Davies, Robertson (1913–1995). Canadian author, dramatist, and critic.

DeForest, J. W. Nineteenth-century American poet.

Degas, Edgar (1834–1917). French painter and sculptor.

de la Mare, Walter (1873–1956). English poet and anthologist.

Dello Joio, Norman. American show-jumping rider and trainer, winner of the 1983 Volvo World Cup.

d'Endrody, Lt. Col. A. L. (d. 1988). Hungarian Olympic three-day eventer and author.

Dent, Anthony. English equestrian historian and journalist.

Dickens, Charles (1812–1870). English novelist.

Dickens, Monica. English novelist, granddaughter of Charles Dickens.

Dickinson, Emily (1830–1886). Americn poet.

Dirga-Tamas (c. 1000). Indian Vedic poet.

Disraeli, Benjamin (1804–1881). British statesman and author.

Dobie, J. Frank (1888–1964). American teacher, historian, and folklorist.

Dorance, Tom. American trainer of western horses.

Dostoyevsky, Fyodor (1821–1881). Russian novelist best known for *Crime and Punishment* and *The Brothers Karamazov*.

Doyle, Sir Arthur Conan (1859–1930). English novelist, creator of Sherlock Holmes.

Drayton, Michael (1563–1631). English poet.

Dryden, John (1631–1700). English poet, dramatist, and critic.

Duncan, Robert. British writer.

Duran, Nina. American artist and writer.

Edgette, Janet Sasson. American clinical and sports psychologist and columnist.

Edinburgh, Prince Philip, Duke of. Consort of Queen Elizabeth II of Great Britain.

Eliot, George. Pen name of Mary Ann Evans (1819–1880), English novelist.

Eliot, T. S. (1888–1965). Anglo-American poet, winner of the 1948 Nobel Prize for literature.

Emerson, Ralph Waldo (1803–1882). American poet, essayist, and philosopher.

Epictetus (c. 50–138). Stoic philosopher.

Evans, Nicholas. British author.

Farley, Walter. American writer best known for his *Black Stallion* series.

Faulkner, William (1897–1962). American novelist and short-story writer, winner of the 1949 Nobel Prize for literature.

Field, Eugene (1850–1895). American poet and journalist.

Fields, W. C. (1880–1946). American film actor.

Fillis, James. Nineteenth-century horse trainer and commentator.

Fleming, Ian (1908–1964). English journalist and novelist, creator of spy James Bond.

Fletcher, Graham. British show jumper, member of the 1976 Montreal Olympics squad.

Florio, John (c. 1553–1625). English writer.

Foote, John Taintor. Nineteenth-century American poet.

Francis, Dick. English ex–steeplechase jockey, now a successful mystery novelist.

Franklin, Benjamin (1706–1790). American statesman and author.

Frazer, Sir James (1854–1941). British anthropologist best known for *The Golden Bough*.

Freud, Sigmund (1856–1939). Austrian physician and a founder of psychoanalysis.

Froissard, Jean. French horseman and author.

Frost, Robert (1875–1963). American poet.

Fuller, Thomas (1608–1661). English clergyman and writer.

Furst, Elizabeth. British equestrian photographer and the author of *Visions of Show Jumping, Visions of Eventing,* and *Visions of Dressage.*

Galsworthy, John (1867–1933). English novelist and dramatist, winner of the 1932 Nobel Prize for literature.

Gambado, Geoffrey. Nineteenth-century English writer.

Gardiner, A. G. Early-twentieth-century British historian.

Gascoigne, George (c. 1539–1577). English dramatist and poet.

Gay, John (1685–1732). English dramatist best known for *The Beggar's Opera.*

Gissing, George (1857–1903). English novelist, critic, and essayist.

Gogol, Nikolay (1809–1852). Russian dramatist, novelist, and short-story writer.

Goldsmith, Oliver (1730?–1774). Anglo-Irish poet and dramatist.

Gordon, Adam Lindsay (1833–1870). British poet.

Gordon-Watson, Mary. British three-day eventer, member of the gold-medal-winning team at the 1972 Munich Olympics.

Grahame, Kenneth (1859–1932). English author of children's books best known for *The Wind in the Willows.*

Graves, John Woodcock (1795–1886). British sportsman whose "John Peel" is foxhunting's most popular song.

Gray, Lendon. American dressage rider, trainer, and writer; member of USET squads for 1980 Alternate Olympics and 1988 Seoul Olympics.

Green, Ben K. (d. 1974). Texan veterinarian and writer.

Greenwood, Grace. Nineteenth-century American poet.

Grey, Zane (1875–1939). American western novelist.

Groves, Lesli K. Editor of *America's Horse* magazine (published by the American Quarter Horse Association).

Gueriniere, François Robichon de la (1688–1751). French horseman, acknowledged originator of the shoulder-in, counter-counter, and flying change of lead.

Guiney, Louise Imogen (1861–1920). American poet.

Guntz, Jean-Louis. Former *ecuyer* (advanced rider) of the *Cadre Noir* of Saumur, France.

Halifax, George Savile, Marquess of (1633–1695). English statesman and man of letters.

Handler, Hans (1912–1974). Former commandant of Vienna's Spanish Riding School, 1964–1974.

Hansen, Joan. American equestrienne and humorist.

Harris, Susan. American horsewoman and writer.

Harte, Bret (1836–1902). American writer of short stories and poetry.

Hawkes, John (b. 1925). American author.

Hawkins, Stephen O. Horse-show judge and official.

Hawthorne, Nathaniel (1804–1864). American novelist and short-story writer.

Hedgpeth, Don. American author and editor.

Heim, Joe. American trainer of cutting horses.

Hemingway, Ernest (1899–1961). American author, winner of the 1954 Nobel Prize for literature.

Henderson, Carolyn, and Lynne Russell. British horsewomen and writers.

Henry, Marguerite. American author of children's stories.

Herbert, Edward, Lord (1583–1648). English soldier, diplomat, and philosopher.

Herbert, George (1593–1633). English poet.

Herbert, Sir A. P. (1890–1971). English humorist, poet, and politician.

Herne, Vicki. Animal behaviorist and author.

Herrick, Robert (1591–1674). English poet.

Herriott, Edouard (1872–1957). French statesman and biographer.

Hervey, John. Twentieth-century turf writer and historian under the pen name Salvadore.

Heywood, John (1497?–1580?). English dramatist.

Hildreth, Samuel Clay. American turf writer.

Holmes, Oliver Wendell, Jr.(1841–1935). Associate justice of the U.S. Supreme Court.

Holmes, Oliver Wendell, Sr.(1809–1894). American author and physician.

Homer (c. 700 B.C.). Greek epic poet best known for *The Iliad* and *The Odyssey*.

Hood, Thomas (1799–1845). English poet.

Housman, A. E. (1859–1936). English poet and scholar.

Hovdey, Jay. American writer.

Howe, Joseph (1804–1873). American writer.

Huber, Mike. American three-day eventer, winner of the 1987 Pan American Games individual and team gold medals.

Hugo-Vidal, Victor. American hunter-seat trainer, judge, and commentator.

Hundt, Sheila Wall. American equestrian writer.

Irving, Washington (1783–1859). American writer.

Isenbart, Hans-Heinrich. Author, television commentator, horse-show judge, and member of the German Olympic Committee.

Issigoris, Alec. British economist.

Jacobson, Patricia, and Marcia Hayes. American equestrian authors.

James, Will (1892–1942). American novelist best known for *Smoky the Cowhorse*.

Jenkins, Rodney. The preeminent professional American show-jumping rider of the 1960s and 1970s (achieving many of his Grand Prix successes aboard Idle Dice).

Johnson, Samuel (1709–1784). English author, lexicographer, and critic.

Jonson, Ben (1572–1637). English dramatist and poet.

Joyce, James (1882–1941). Irish novelist, short-story writer, and poet, best known for *Ulysses* and *Finnegan's Wake*.

Kahn, Roger. American journalist and essayist.

Karr, Elizabeth. Nineteenth-century American equestrienne and writer.

Keats, John (1795–1821). English poet.

Khrushchev, Nikita (1894–1971). Soviet leader, premier of USSR 1957–1964.

Kingsley, Charles (1819–1875). English author and clergyman.

Kipling, Rudyard (1865–1936). English author and poet, winner of the 1907 Nobel Prize for literature.

Klimke, Reiner. German dressage rider, six-time world champion and six-time Olympic gold medalist.

Klinkenborg, Verlyn. American journalist and author.

Knowles, James Sheridan (1784–1862). English poet and dramatist.

Kottas-Heldenberg, Arthur. Former *Oberberreiter* (chief rider) of Vienna's Spanish Riding School.

Krantz, Judith. American novelist.

Kunffy, Charles de. American dressage author and commentator.

Kursinski, Anne. American show jumper, member of the 1988 and 1992 USET Olympic squads.

Kyd, Thomas (1558–1594). English dramatist, best known for *The Spanish Tragedy*.

Kyle, Jack. American western trainer, member of the American Quarter Horse Association Hall of Fame.

Lanier, Sidney (1841–1881). American poet.

la Tour d'Auvergne, Princess Patricia Galvin de. American three-day event and dressage rider.

Lawrence, D. H. (1885–1930). English author.

Lea, Tom. American writer and western historian.

Leacock, Stephen (1869–1944). Canadian humorist.

Lear, Edward (1812–1888). English writer known for his limericks and nonsense verse.

Lewis, C. S. (1898–1963). English novelist, critic, and essayist.

Lewis, Joe E. (1902–1971). American comedian.

Lewis, Meriwether (1774–1808). American explorer.

l'Hotte, Gen. Alexis. Nineteenth-century French horseman and commentator.

Licart, Jean (d. 1965). French cavalry officer and horseman.

Lichtenberg, Georg Christoph (1742–1799). German writer.

Linderman, Bill. American rodeo cowboy, 1954 all-around champion.

Lindsay, Vachel (1879–1931). American poet.

Littauer, Vladimir S. (d. 1989). Russian-born cavalry officer and author, among the innovators of forward-seat riding.

Ljungquist, Bengt (d. 1978). Former coach, United States Equestrian Team dressage squad.

Llewellyn, Col. Sir Harry. British show jumper; member of Olympic team gold medal (1952) and team bronze medal (1956) squads.

Lofting, Hugh (1886–1947). English-born American writer of children's books, best known for *Doctor Dolittle*.

Long, Earl (d. 1960). Governor of Louisiana 1939–1940, 1948–1952, 1956–1960.

Longfellow, Henry Wadsworth (1807–1882). American poet.

Lovelace, Richard (1618–1657?). English poet.

Luther, Martin (1483–1546). German religious leader.

Lyons, John. Western trainer whose clinics and symposia draw thousands of spectators every year.

Macaulay, Thomas Babington, Lord (1800–1859). British historian and man of letters.

Mackay-Smith, Alexander (d. 1998). American editor, author, and horse-sports official.

MacLeish, Archibald (1892–1982). American poet, winner of the Pulitzer Prize in 1933, 1953, and 1959.

Mahan, Larry. Horse trainer and former all-around rodeo cowboy champion.

Mannes, Marya (1904–1990). American poet and essayist.

Mao Tse-tung (1893–1976). Chinese political leader.

Marcy, Capt. Randolph B. Nineteenth-century American military officer and historian.

Markham, Beryl (1902–1986). English aviator and author, best known for *West with the Night.*

Markham, Gervase (1568?–1637). English author and poet.

Martin, Pepper. American baseball player.

Marx, Groucho (1895–1977). American humorist and actor.

Masefield, John (1878–1967). English poet, dramatist, and novelist.

Masters, Edgar Lee (1868–1950). American poet and novelist.

McClung, Cooky. American humorist and columnist.

McDonald, Marjorie B. American ex–Master of Fox Hounds of the Meadowbrook [Long Island, N.Y.] Hunt.

McGreevy, Paul. British veterinarian and animal behaviorist now living in Australia.

McGuane, Thomas. American novelist and essayist.

Mellon, Paul (d. 1999). American philanthropist and Thoroughbred owner and breeder.

Melville, Herman (1819–1891). American author best known for *Moby-Dick*.

Menino, Holly. Author of *Forward Motion: World Class Riders and the Horses Who Carry Them.*

Meredith, George (1828–1909). English novelist, poet, and critic.

Michener, James (1907–1997). American author.

Midkiff, Mary D. American writer and entrepreneur.

Millar, Ian. Canadian show jumper, winner of 1988 and 1989 Volvo World Cups.

Milton, John (1608–1674). English poet, best known for *Paradise Lost.*

Montagu, Lady Mary Wortley (1689–1762). English writer.

Montague, Sarah. English-born American writer and editor.

Montaigne, Michel de (1533–1592). French essayist.

Morris, George H. Show-jumping rider, preeminent hunter-seat equitation trainer and author; member of the team silver medal squad at the 1960 Rome Olympics.

Morris, William (1834–1896). English poet, artist, and designer.

Mr. Ed. The "talking horse" of the 1960s television series.

Munro, H. H. (1870–1916). Writer of short stories under the pen name Saki.

Murphy, Dennis. American show jumper, member of the USET 1976 Olympic and 1975 Pan American Games squads.

Müsler, Wilhelm. German horseman and writer.

Mutch, R. W. (d. 1999). American rider, trainer, graphic designer, and cartoonist.

Newcastle, William Cavendish, Duke of. Seventeenth-century courtier and horseman, riding instructor to Charles II.

Norton, Caroline Elizabeth Sheridan (1808–1877). English writer and social reformer.

O'Hara, Mary (1885–1980). American author of children's stories, best known for *My Friend Flicka*.

Oliveira, Nuno. Preeminent Portuguese dressage master.

Page, Michael O. American three-day eventer, winner of the individual bronze medal at the 1968 Mexico City Olympics.

Palmer, Joe. American sportswriter and journalist.

Parkman, Francis (1823–1893). American historian.

Penn, William (1644–1718). English-born American political and religious leader.

Pessoa, Nelson. Brazilian show jumper, member of four Olympic squads; father of show jumper Rodrigo Pessoa, 1998 World Cup and 1998 World Equestrian Games champion.

Phillips, Capt. Mark. Former British three-day eventer, now coach of the USET's three-day squad.

Pierpont, J. Nineteenth-century American writer.

Pinch, Dorothy Henderson (d. 1966).

Plato (c. 427–348 B.C.). Greek philosopher.

Pliny the Elder (23?–79). Roman naturalist.

Plutarch (76?–c. 120). Greek essayist and biographer, best known for *Lives*.

Podhajsky, Alois. Commandant of Vienna's Spanish Riding School from 1939 to 1964.

Polo, Marco (1254?–1324?). Italian explorer.

Pope, Alexander (1688–1744). English poet and critic.

Praed, Winthrop Mackworth (1802–1839). English poet.

Price, Steven D. Equestrian author and journalist.

Prince, Eleanor F., and Gaydell M. Collier. American equestrian writers.

Prudent, Katie Monahan. American show-jumping rider and trainer, member of 1980 Alternate Olympics team.

Publicus Syrus (first century B.C.). Roman epigramist.

Quintus Smyrnaeus (c. 100 B.C.). Roman poet.

Rabelais, François (c. 1490–1553). French author, best known for *Gargantua and Pantagruel*.

Rarey, James. Nineteenth-century horse trainer.

Raspe, Rudolph (1737–1794). German writer, best known for *The Travels of Baron Munchausen*.

Rees, Lucy. British equine behaviorist and writer.

Renoir, Jean (1894–1979). French film director, son of painter Pierre-Auguste Renoir.

Richter, Judy. American hunter-seat trainer and writer.

Riley, James Whitcomb (1849–1916). American poet.

Roberts, Monty. Trainer whose *The Man Who Listens to Horses* was a 1998 best-seller.

Rogers, Roy (d. 1999). American cowboy film and TV actor.

Rogers, Will (1879–1935). American humorist and actor.

Rose, Pete. American trainer of western horses.

Rosenthal, Kip. Trainer of hunters, jumpers, and equitation horses and riders.

Rossetti, Christina (1830–1895). English poet.

Rubin, Sam. American Thoroughbred racehorse owner.

Runyan, Damon (1880–1946). American journalist and short-story writer.

Ruskin, John (1819–1900). English writer, artist, and social critic.

Salinger, J. D. American novelist and short-story writer, best known for *The Catcher in the Rye*.

Salten, Felix. Austrian author, best known for *Bambi*.

Sandburg, Carl (1878–1967). American poet and biographer.

Santini, Piero (1881–1960). Italian writer whose books and lectures popularized the forward-seat system of riding.

Sassoon, Siegfried (1886–1947). English poet and novelist.

Savoie, Jane. American dressage rider and author.

Scott, Sir Walter (1771–1832). Scottish poet and novelist.

Self, Margaret Cabell (d. 1996). American horsewoman and writer.

Service, Robert W. (1874–1958). Canadian author and poet.

Seunig, Waldemar. German horseman and writer.

Sewell, Anna (1820–1878). English writer best known for *Black Beauty*.

Shakespeare, William (1564–1616). English dramatist.

Shapiro, Neal. American show jumper, winner of the individual bronze medal at the 1972 Munich Olympics.

Shaw, George Bernard (1856–1950). Irish dramatist, critic, and social reformer, winner of the 1925 Nobel Prize for literature.

Sherbrooke, Robert Lowe, Lord (1811–1892). English sportsman.

Sidney, Sir Philip (1554–1586). English author, diplomat, and courtier, known as the paradigm of Renaissance chivalry.

Sigourney, Lydia Huntley (1791–1865). American poet and writer.

Simpson, George Gaylord. British anthropologist.

Sitwell, Sir Osbert (1892–1969). English writer and poet.

Slater, Joy. American horsewoman; first woman to win the Maryland Hunt Cup steeplechase.

Smart, Christopher (1722–1771). English poet and journalist.

Smiley, Jane. American author, winner of a 1992 Pulitzer Prize.

Smith, Bradley. American writer and photographer.

Smith, Cecil (d. 1999). Preeminent American polo player.

Smith, Red (Walter W.) (1905–1982). American newspaper c olumnist, winner of a 1976 Pulitzer Prize.

Smith, Robyn. American jockey, one of the first women to succeed as a professional race rider.

Smith, Sharon B. American author and print and broadcast journalist.

Somerville, E. O. (1861–1949), and Martin Ross (1862–1915; pen name of Violet Martin). Irish novelists.

St. John, Henry, Viscount Bolingbroke (1678–1751). English statesman, orator, and man of letters.

Steffens, Lincoln (1866–1936). American journalist.

Steinbeck, John (1902–1968). American writer best known for *The Grapes of Wrath,* for which he won a 1939 Pulitzer Prize and the 1962 Nobel Prize for literature.

Steinkraus, William. Show-jumping rider, author, editor, and USET official; winner of the individual gold medal at the 1968 Mexico City Olympics (the first such victory for a USET rider).

Sterne, Laurence (1713–1768). English novelist, best known for *Tristram Shandy*.

Stevenson, Robert Louis (1850–1894). Scottish author and poet.

Surrey, Henry Howard, Earl of (1517?–1547). English poet.

Surtees, Robert Smith. Nineteenth-century English humorist, creator of the foxhunting character John Jorrocks.

Swift, Jonathan (1667–1745). Anglo-Irish author and satirist, best known for *Gulliver's Travels*.

Swift, Sally. American trainer, developer of the "centered riding" system.

Synge, John Millington (1871–1909). Irish dramatist.

Taylor, Bayard (1825–1878). American writer and traveler.

Taylor, Elizabeth. American actress; star of *National Velvet.*

Tellington-Jones, Linda. American animal behaviorist; founder of TTEAM (Tellington-Jones Equine Awareness Method).

Tennyson, Alfred, Lord (1809–1892). English poet.

Tesio, Federico. Italian breeder of Thoroughbred horses.

Thompson, James (1700–1748). Scottish-born English poet.

Topsel, Edward. Eighteenth-century naturalist.

Trollope, Anthony (1815–1882). English novelist.

Trotsky, Leon (1879–1940). Russian revolutionary.

Tuchman, Barbara. American historian, winner of Pulitzer Prizes in 1962 and 1971.

Turner, Chubby. American trainer of cutting horses.

Twain, Mark. Pen name of Samuel L. Clemens (1835–1910), American author best known for *Tom Sawyer* and *Huckleberry Finn.*

Tyler, John (1790–1862). Tenth president of the United States.

Virgil (70–19 B.C.). Roman poet, author of *The Aeneid.*

Wadsworth, William P. Ex–Master of Fox Hounds of the Genesee Valley [Geneseo, N.Y.] Hunt.

Wallace, Lew (1827–1905). American military officer and author, best known for *Ben-Hur*.

Waller, Edmund (1606–1687). English poet.

Wanless, Mary. British trainer and writer.

Warwick, Frances, Countess of. Early-twentieth-century English aristocrat.

Weaver, Jason. American jockey.

Welch, Buster. American trainer of cutting horses.

Wellington, Arthur Wellesley, Duke of (1769–1852). British military and political leader.

West, Jessamyn (d. 1986). American author.

White, William Allen (1868–1944). American author and newspaper editor.

White-Mullins, Anna-Jane. American trainer and author.

Whitman, Walt (1819–1892). American poet, best known for *Leaves of Grass*.

Whyte-Melville, G. J. (1821–1878). English novelist and poet.

Wilcox, Ella Wheeler (1850–1919). English poet.

Wilde, Oscar (1854–1900). Irish dramatist, poet, and essayist.

Williams, Jimmy (d. 1993). American rider, innovative trainer, and movie stuntman.

Wister, Owen (1860–1938). American novelist best known for *The Virginians*.

Wittgenstein, Ludwig (1889–1951). Austrian philosopher.

Wodehouse, P. G. (1881–1975). English writer best known for his Bertie Wooster and Jeeves stories.

Wofford, James C. American three-day eventer, member of four USET Olympic squads and winner of two silver medals; former president of the American Horse Shows Association.

Wolf, A. London. Astute observer of horse sports (and wife of the author).

Wolfe, Tom (b. 1931). American novelist and man of letters.

Woolfe, Raymond, Jr. American photographer and writer.

Wordsworth, William (1770–1850). English poet.

Wright, Gordon (1903–1989). American trainer largely responsible for the development of hunter-seat horsemanship.

Wyatt, Sir Thomas (1503–1542). English poet and statesman.

Xenophon (c. 430–355 B.C.). Greek historian and author of the first surviving riding treatise.

Yeats, William Butler (1865–1939). Irish poet and dramatist, winner of the 1923 Nobel Prize for literature.

Youngman, Henny (d. 1998). American comedian.

Zarzyski, Paul. American "cowboy poet."

Index

K

L